ANCIENT INDIAN TRADITION & MYTHOLOGY

Translated by

A BOARD OF SCHOLARS

Edited by

G.P. Bhatt

VOLUME **77**

ANCIENT INDIAN TRADITION AND MYTHOLOGY

Mahāpurāṇas *Translated into English*
Gen. Ed. Dr. G.C. Tripathi
Founder Eds. Late J.L. Shastri and Late G.P. Bhatt

PUBLISHED VOLUMES

Vols. 1-4 ŚIVA PURĀṆA *Tr.* J.L. Shastri

Vols. 5-6 LIṄGA PURĀṆA *Tr.* J.L. Shastri

Vols. 7-11 BHĀGAVATA PURĀṆA *Tr.* G.V. Tagare

Vols. 12-14 GARUḌA PURĀṆA *Tr.* J.L. Shastri

Vols. 15-19 NĀRADA PURĀṆA *Tr.* G.V. Tagare

Vols. 20-21 KŪRMA PURĀṆA *Tr.* G.V. Tagare

Vols. 22-26 BRAHMĀṆḌA PURĀṆA *Tr.* G.V. Tagare

Vols. 27-30 AGNI PURĀṆA *Tr.* N. Gangadharan

Vols. 31-32 VARĀHA PURĀṆA *Tr.* S. Venkitasubramonia Iyer

Vols. 33-36 BRAHMA PURĀṆA *Tr.* J.L. Shastri

Vols. 37-38 VĀYU PURĀṆA *Tr.* G.V. Tagare

Vols. 39-48 PADMA PURĀṆA *Tr.* N.A. Deshpande

Vols. 49-71 SKANDA PURĀṆA *Ed.* G.P. Bhatt,
Tr. & Annot. Shridhar Balooni & Pratosh Panda

Vols. 72-73 VĀMANA PURĀṆA
Tr. & Annot. R.S. Shiva Ganesha Murthy

Vols. 74-76 GAṆEŚA PURĀṆA *Tr. & Annot.* Greg Bailey

Vols. 77-82 BRAHMAVAIVARTA PURĀṆA *Tr. & Annot.* G.P. Bhatt

PURĀṆAS UNDER PREPARATION

Viṣṇu Purāṇa • Harivaṃśa Purāṇa • Bhaviṣya Purāṇa • Matsya Purāṇa • Devī Bhāgavata Purāṇa • Kālika Purāṇa • Mārkaṇḍeya Purāṇa • Viṣṇudharmottara Purāṇa

Brahmavaivarta Purāṇa

Part- I

Brahma Khaṇḍa

Translated and annotated by

G.P. Bhatt

MOTILAL BANARSIDASS PUBLISHERS
PRIVATE LIMITED • DELHI

First Edition: ***Delhi, 2016***

ISBN: 978-81-208-4029-4

MOTILAL BANARSIDASS
41 U.A. Bungalow Road, Jawahar Nagar, Delhi 110 007
8 Mahalaxmi Chamber, 22 Bhulabhai Desai Road, Mumbai 400 026
120 Royapettah High Road, Mylapore, Chennai 600 004
236, 9th Main III Block, Jayanagar, Bangaluru 560 011
8 Camac Street, Kolkata 700 017
Ashok Rajpath, Patna 800 004
Chowk, Varanasi 221 001

UNESCO COLLECTION OF REPRESENTATIVE WORKS—*Indian Series*
This book has been accepted in the Indian Translation Series of the UNESCO Collection of Representative Works, jointly sponsored by the United Nations Educational, Scientific and Cultural Organization (UNESCO) and the Government of India

MLBD Cataloging-in-Publication Data
Brahmavaivarta Purana (Part-I)
Brahma Khanda by G.P. Bhatt
Includes Notes
ISBN: 978-81-208-4029-4
I. Hinduism II. Purana III. Brahmavaivarta
IV. Brahma Khanda V. Bhatt, G.P.

Printed in India

by RP Jain at NAB Printing Unit,
A-44, Naraina Industrial Area, Phase I, New Delhi–110028
and published by JP Jain for Motilal Banarsidass Publishers (P) Ltd,
41 U.A. Bungalow Road, Jawahar Nagar, Delhi-110007

PUBLISHER'S NOTE

The purest gems lie hidden in the bottom of the ocean or in the depth of rocks. One has to dive into the ocean or delve into the rocks to find them out. Similarly, truth lies concealed in the language which with the passage of time has become obsolete. Man has to learn that language before he discovers that truth.

But he has neither the means nor the leisure to embark on that course. We have, therefore, planned to help him acquire knowledge by an easier course. We have started the series of Ancient Indian Tradition and Mythology in English Translation. Our goal is to universalize knowledge through the most popular international medium of expression. The publication of the Purāṇas in English Translation is a step towards that goal.

Acknowledgement

It is our pleasant duty to put on record our sincere thanks to Dr. R.N. Dandekar and the UNESCO authorities for their kind encouragement and valuable help in the publication of the volumes in this series.

NOTE OF THE GENERAL EDITOR

With a certain mingle of the feelings of joy and sorrow we are presenting herewith one of the most important Purāṇas in its English translation. While being happy to bring this work to light, we are deeply sorry to note that the translator of this work Dr. G.P. Bhatt, one of the best experts on Purāṇic lore who has been associated with this our grand endeavour of AITM for a long time, is unfortunately no more to see the fruit of his labour in print. During his life time he could finish the translation of only half of this Purāṇa, i.e. the first two khaṇḍas (Brahma & Prakṛti), whereas the other two still need to be translated.

The Purāṇakāra has created the title of his work from a technical term of the Advaita Vedānta. '*Vivarta*' is used to describe a phenomenon which we perceive and experience as *real* but which in its substance is totally different from it. According to Advaita Vedānta this whole creation is a '*vivarta*' of Brahman, which is to say that intrinsically every phenomenon and every object is essentially and substantially Brahman but it appears to us in various universal forms. Brahman is the ultimate and the only reality of everything that we perceive and experience.

Our Purāṇa thus seeks to stress the point that all objects of the world, all creatures and even the divine beings about which it speaks are ultimately manifestations of Brahman who or which is none else than Kṛṣṇa and his Śaktis, though they may not appear as such.

The word '*vivarta*' in this technical sense has been made popular especially by Śaṅkarācārya in his exposition of the Brahmasūtras. It appears therefore likely that the author of the Purāṇa was well acquainted with this great philosopher and his works.

Our Purāṇa does not choose to elaborate any one particular subject or theme, nor has it any single plan of narration, in fact few Purāṇas have it.

Our Purāṇa can very well be described as a quadrology of four completely independent works, however with a marked Krishnaite bias permeated through the whole text. Whereas this first section (Brahmakhaṇḍa) mainly (though not exclusively) deals with the earlier manifestation of the creation from god Brahma-Kṛṣṇa, the other three are more coherent, dealing with god Ganeśa, five main Goddesses and exploits of Kṛṣṇa, along with Rādhā.

The most important section of this Purāṇa for which it is known and also held in high esteem by the Gauḍīya Vaiṣṇavas especially, is its fourth section in which the person of Rādhā is depicted in its full glory. There is no other Purāṇa among the major eighteen ones which depicts the character, personality and the sportive activities of Rādhā with Kṛṣṇa. Not even Bhāgavata Purāṇa mentions her name in its Xth Skandha which is solely devoted to the exploits of Kṛṣṇa. The only other text which describes the love sports of Rādhā and her female mates with Kṛṣṇa is *Garga Saṃhitā*. But it does not have the status of a Purāṇa.

Although stray references to Rādhā can be traced back to the 1st c. of the current era (first mention in the *Gathāsaptaśtī* of Hāla) yet it is in fact in this Purāṇa as well as in the *Gītagovinda* of Jayadeva (12th c.) that she receives her true personality in flesh and blood. But whereas the Rādhā of Gītagovinda is a shy, love-lorn maiden not married to Kṛṣṇa, the Rādhā of our Purāṇa is the first wife of Kṛṣṇa, also his eternal consort, well versed in love games.

Gītagovinda was composed by an Oriya poet, and the section on Kṛṣṇa of our Purāṇa seems to have been composed in Bengal because the concept of Rādhā as a married woman elder in age to Kṛṣṇa is still prevalent in that region. In any case, the provenance of the present reworked version of our

Purāṇa appears to be the Eastern part of India in all likelihood because not only a few sub-castes of Bengal find mention in its first Khaṇḍa, but also the holy river Virajā flowing through north Odisha is referred to in the very beginning of fourth section. The glorification of Mother Goddess in its third section, her various forms and exploits mentioned in BVP also point towards this direction, which is corroborated by a detailed description of the ceremony of the marriage between Kṛṣṇa and Rukmiṇī (IVth Khaṇḍa) which is not substantially different from the rites that take place today in central-eastern and Eastern India. This also point towards its relatively late origin, much later than the classical age. By the way, this also gives us some clue about the approximate date of the BVP which must be around 10th-12th c. or a little later.

I hope that the present translation of this Purāṇa finds the same warm welcome with the scholars, especially with those who are interested in the development of Kṛṣṇa cult, which they have accorded to the previous volumes of this series.

—**Dr. G.C. Tripathi**

CONTENTS

Publisher's Note v

Note of the General Editor vii

Abbreviations xiii

Introduction xvii

BRAHMAVAIVARTA PURĀṆA

Brahma Khaṇḍa

Part-I

Invocation 1

Introductory 2

1. Contents of the Purāṇa 2
2. Exposition about the Supreme Brahman 8
3. The Exposition about Creation 11
4. Manifestation of Minor Gods 19
5. The Periods of Time and the Creation of Goloka and Rādhā 22
6. Eulogy of Śiva on Kṛṣṇa and Merits of Worship of Śiva 28
7. The Creation of the Worlds 34
8. The Creation of the Sages and the Mutual Curses of Brahmā and Nārada 36
9. The Further Creation of Other Beings 41
10. The Origin of the Different Castes 49
11. The Greatness of a Devotee of Viṣṇu 63

12. The Birth of Nārada as a *Gandharva* 68
13. The Lamentation of Mālāvatī, a *Gandharva* Woman 72
14. The Dialogue between Mālāvatī and Viṣṇu and the Greatness of Kṛṣṇa 79
15. The Dialogue between Mālāvat and Kālapuruṣa 85
16. The Conversation between Viṣṇu and Mālatī on Medical Treatment 90
17. The Dialogue between Lord Viṣṇu and the Gods and the Greatness of Lord Viṣṇu 97
18. The Revival of the *Gandharva* and Mālatī's Eulogy of the Supreme God 103
19. Eulogy on (Lords) Viṣṇu and Śiva 107
20. The Narration of the Story of Upabarhana 115
21. The Release of Nārada from the Curse 120
22. The Etymology of the Names of the Sons of Brahmā 125
23. The Dialogue between Brahmā and Nārada 128
24. The Dialogue of Brahmā and Nārada about Mundane Existence 132
25. Nārada's Visit to Kailāśa 136
26. The Dialogue between Śiva and Nārada about Daily Practices 139
27. The Instruction about Daily Practices 147
28. The Form of Brahman, Vaikuṇṭha, etc. 151
29. The Query of Nārada about the Supreme Being Lord Kṛṣṇa 157
30. The Eulogy Glorifying Lord Kṛṣṇa 158

Notes 161

ABBREVIATIONS

Common and self-evident abbreviations such as Ch(s)—Chapter(s), p—page, pp.—pages, v—verse, vv—verses, Ftn—Footnote, Hist. Ind. Philo.—History of Indian Philosophy are not included in this list.

ABORI	*Annals of the Bhandarkar Oriental Research Institute,* Poona
AGP	S.M. Ali's The Geography of *Purāṇas,* PPH, New Delhi, 1973
AIHT	*Ancient Indian Historical Tradition,* F.E. Pargiter, Motilal Banarsidass (MLBD), Delhi
AITM	*Ancient Indian Tradition and Mythology Series,* MLBD, Delhi
AP	*Agni Purāṇa,* Guru Mandal Edition (GM), Calcutta, 1957
Arch. S. Rep.	*Archaeological Survey Report*
AV	*Atharva Veda,* Svādhyāya Maṇḍal, Aundh
BdP	*Brahmāṇḍa Purāṇa,* MLBD, Delhi 1973
BG	*Bhagavadgītā*
BhP	*Bhāgavata Purāṇa,* Bhagavat Vidyapeeth, Ahmedabad
Br	*Brāhmaṇa* (preceded by name such as Śatapatha)
BsP	*Bhaviṣya Purāṇa,* Vishnu Shastrī Bapat, Wai
BVP	*Brahma Vaivarta Purāṇa,* GM, 1955-57
CC	*Caturvarga Cintāmaṇi* by Hemādri

CVS	*Caraṇa Vyūha Sūtra* by Śaunaka, Commentary by Mahīdāsa
DB	*Devī Bhāgavata, GM,* 1960-57
De or GDAMI	*The Geographical Dictionary of Ancient and Mediaeval India,* N.L. De, Oriental Reprint, Delhi, 1971
DhS	*Dharma Sūtra* (preceded by the author's name such as Gautama)
ERE	*Encyclopaedia of Religion and Ethics* by Hastings
GP	*Garuḍa Purāṇa,* ed. R.S. Bhattacharya, Chowkhamba, Varanasi, 1964
GS	*Gṛhya Sūtra* (preceded by the name of the author such as Āpastamba)
HD	*History of Dharma Śāstra,* P.V. Kane, G.O.S.
IA	*The Indian Antiquary*
IHQ	*The Indian Historical Quarterly*
JP	*Purāṇa* (Journal of the Kashiraj Trust), Varanasi
KA	*Kauṭilya Arthaśāstra*
KP	*Kūrma Purāṇa,* Veṅkaṭeśvara Press Edn., Bombay; also Kashiraj Trust Edn., Varanasi, 1971
LP	*Liṅga Purāṇa,* GM, 1960; also MLBD, Delhi, 1981
Manu	*Manusmṛti*
Mbh	*Mahābhārata,* Gītā Press, Gorakhpur, VS 2014
MkP	*Mārkaṇḍeya Purāṇa*
MN	*Mahābhārata Nāmānukramaṇi,* Gita Press, Gorakhpur, VS 2016
MtP	*Matsya Purāṇa,* GM, 1954
MW	Monier Williams' *Sanskrit-English Dictionary,* MLBD, Delhi 1976

NP	*Nāradīya* or *Nārada Purāṇa*, Veṅkaṭeśvara Press, Bombay
PCK	*Bhāratavarṣīya Prācīna Caritrakośa*, Siddheshwar Shastri, Poona, 1968
PdP	*Padma Purāṇa*, GM, 1957-59
PE	*Purāṇic Encyclopaedia*, V. Mani, English version, MLBD, Delhi, 1975
PR or PRHRC	*Puranic Records on Hindu Rites and Customs*, R.C. Hazra, Calcutta, 1948
ṚV	*Ṛg-Veda*, Svādhyāya Maṇḍal, Aundh
Śat Br	*Śatapatha Brāhmaṇa*
SC or SMC	*Smṛti Candrikā* by Devanna Bhaṭṭa
SEP	*Studies in Epics and Purāṇas*, A.D. Psalkar, Bharatiya Vidya Bhavan (BVB), Bombay
SkP	*Skanda Purāṇa*
SP	*Śiva Purāṇa*
VāP	*Vāyu Purāṇa*
VR	*Vālmīki Rāmāyaṇa*
VdP	*Viṣṇudharmottara Purāṇa*
VmP	*Vāmana Purāṇa*
VP	*Viṣṇu Purāṇa*
VrP	*Varāha Purāṇa*

INTRODUCTION*

It is believed that the study of the Purāṇas is beneficial to the knowledge of the *vedas.* As the *Mahābhārata*[1] states, the *veda* should be supplemented with the Itihāsa and Purāṇa, for the *veda* is afraid of being hurt by a person who is not well-versed (in the mythological and traditional lore). The traditionalists take the word Purāṇa to mean the Purāṇic texts like *Matsya, Kūrma,* etc. and attach to them great authority and veneration. They hold that the Purāṇic texts are repositories of very ancient knowledge because they have been referred to in the *Bṛhadāraṇyaka Upaniṣad.*[2] Modern Scholars dispute this claim and say that not the extant Purāṇic texts but some parts of the *vedas* which preserve very old traditions, alluded to in other places of the *vedas,* are referred to in the *Bṛhadāraṇyaka Upaniṣad,* as the Purāṇa. They quote, in support of their thesis, Śaṅkarācārya's interpretation of the said passage of the *Bṛhadāraṇyaka Upaniṣad: "Mythology,* such as "The universe was in the beginning unmanifest' etc.".[3]

It is true that the extant Purāṇa texts are much posterior to the early Upaniṣads and, hence, could not have been referred to in the *Bṛhadāraṇyaka Upaniṣad.* But this position does not reduce the usefulness and authority of the Purāṇas. The Purāṇa is not a particular set of texts, it is a branch of ancient Indian learning, a class of ancient Indian literature. The nucleus of

---

*Courtesy : *Brahmavaivarta Purāna of Kṛṣṇa Dvaipāyana Vyāsa* (Original Sanskrit text with Introduction in Sanskrit and English, and alphabetical Index by Prof. Satkari Mukhopadhyaya) in 2 Parts, Ed. by Acharya Jagdish Lal Shastri, MLBD, 1984 (Reprint 2004).

this branch of class existed in the body of the *vedas*, which gradually developed into the *Purāṇasaṃhitā* and then into the present *Mahāpurāṇas*, *Upapurāṇas*, and later apocrypha. The authority of the Purāṇa, as mentioned in the *Mahābhārata*, is vested in this whole class. In this way, we can reconcile the interpretation of Śaṅkarācārya[4] with the classical five characteristics of the Purāṇas, e.g. primary creation (*sarga*), dissolution (*pratisarga*), genealogy (*vaṁśa*), ages of Manus (*manvantara*) and history of Royal dynasties and some illustrious personages (*vaṁśānucarita*).

There is no controversy about *Brahmavaivartapurāṇa*'s being a major Purāṇa (*Mahāpurāṇa*).

The *Brahmavaivartapurāṇa* figures as the tenth in the traditional lists of the Purāṇas.

The *Brahmavaivartapurāṇa* is divided into four parts called *khaṇḍas*, comprising 267 chapters. The *khaṇḍas* are : *Brahmakhaṇḍa* : 30 chapters, *Prakṛtikhaṇḍa* : 67 chapters, *Gaṇapatikhaṇḍa* : 46 chapters and *Śrikṛṣṇajanmakhaṇḍa* : 133 chapters.

The *Matsya*[5] and *Nāradapurāṇa*[6] describe the total number of verses of the *Brahmavaivartapurāṇa* as 18,000. The *Brahmavaivarta*[7] itself mentions the same number. But the actual counting of the verses of the Purāṇa, now available, gives a total of little over 20,500 verses.

The *Brahmavaivarta*[8] rejects the traditional five characteristics as covering the *Upapurāṇas* only and holds that ten topics are dealt with in a Mahāpurāṇa : they are : primary creation (*sṛsti*), secondary creation (*visṛṣṭi*), stability of the creation (*sthiti*), protection (*pālana*), desire for work (*karmavāsanā*), information about different Manus (*Manu-vārtā*), description of the final destruction of the world (*pralaya-varṇanā*), showing the way to emancipation (*mokṣa-nirūpaṇa*), discourses on Hari (*Harikirtana*), and discourses on other gods (*devakirtana*).[9] The purpose of this substitution of list of topics in the *Bhāgavata* and *Brahmavaivarta* has been discussed by Dr. R.C. Hazra and his opinion on this point deserves serious consideration.[10]

A complete table of contents (*anukramaṇikā*) is included in the chapter 132 of the *Śrikṛṣṇajanmakhaṇḍa.*

It is well known that the *Brahmavaivarta* is a Vaiṣṇavite Purāṇa and the sole objective of the work is to glorify the life and achievements of Śrī Kṛṣṇa, an incarnation of Viṣṇu and his Śakti Rādhā. Many episodes and topics have been interwoven to embellish the main theme of the work. In this Purāṇa, Kṛṣṇa is not simply an incarnation, he is far superior to and even creator of Prakṛti. He is God above all gods.

Part I, i.e., *Brahmakhaṇḍa* deals with the creation of the universe including the gods and animate and inanimate beings by Brahman, the creator God, who is, according to this Purāṇa, none other than a manifestation of Kṛṣṇa and acts under the guidance of the latter.

Part II, i.e., *Prakṛtikhaṇḍa* deals with Prakṛti, the primordial matter. According to this Purāṇa, Prakṛti is not inert as she is conceived by the Sāṅkhya philosophy, but is intelligent; she is the primary goddess of creation.[11] In compliance with Kṛṣṇa's desire, she is manifested as the five goddesses,[12] viz. Durgā, Rādhā, Lakṣmī, Sarasvatī, and Sāvitrī.[13] Many stories about these deities have been narrated and rituals for their worship described in this part.

Part III, i.e., *Gaṇapatikhaṇḍa* narrates many legends about Gaṇeśa, the elephant-headed god, widely worshipped throughout India and even outside. Though named *Gaṇapatikhaṇḍa,* this part deals with the birth and life of both sons of Śiva, viz. Gaṇeśa and Skanda Kārttikeya. According to this Purāṇa, Gaṇeśa is also a manifestation of Kṛṣṇa. Hence, there is no mention of Gāṇapatya sects who worshipped Gaṇeśa as the Supreme Godhead. The variations in the images of this deity, found in literature and on icons find no mention in the Purāṇa.

Part IV, i.e., *Śrīkṛṣṇajanmakhaṇḍa* is the most important of all books of this Purāṇa. It deals not only with the birth of Kṛṣṇa, as signified by the title, but also his whole life, especially his battles and love dalliances with the cowherdesses (*gopīs*), in particular, with Rādhā. Rādhā, who is not even mentioned in the major Vaiṣṇava Purāṇas like *Bhāgavata, Viṣṇu,* and

Harivaṃśa, has risen in this Purāṇa, to a great importance. It is interesting to note that she is depicted here as a married wife of Kṛṣṇa.[14]

Authority of the Text

Much can be discussed about the authority of extant *Brahmavaivartapurāṇa*. The authority of the Purāṇa is apparently established, because it is mentioned in older texts *Matsya*, *Nārada*, etc.[15] But there exists a great discrepancy between the *Brahmavaivarta* as mentioned in the *Matsya* and *Nārada* purāṇa and the text that is available now. The *Matsyapurāṇa* says that the story of the *Brahmavaivarta* has been narrated by Sāvarṇi to Nārada, it includes the episode of Brahmavarāha, and it comprises 18,000 verses. But, we do not find even the name of Sāvarṇi in the *Brahmavaivarta* now extant, nor the episode of Brahmavarāha can be traced to it. It can, therefore, be inferred that the original form of the Purāṇa has undergone a great change. It is also interesting to note that only 30 lines out of 1500, quoted from the *Brahmavaivarta* in medieval *smṛti-nibandhas*, like *Smṛticandrikā*, *Caturvargacintāmaṇi*, *Kālanirṇaya*, *Smṛtitattva*, *Varṣakriyākaumudi*, etc. can be traced to the extant text.[16] It may, therefore, be presumed that a considerable part of the older text, containing genealogies, geographical descriptions, etc. has been purged and replaced by later compositions which suit the purpose of Vaiṣṇava sects. This transformation has diminished the authority of the Purāṇa to a great extent.

Date of Composition

It is not easy to determine, with any amount of certainty, the date of composition of the *Brahmavaivartapurāṇa*, because it contains both ancient and medieval materials. It is then obvious that there would be difference of opinion among scholars about the date of this Purāṇa. Wilson's view[17] that the *Brahmavaivartapurāṇa* was composed after the Mohammadan conquest of Northern India, need not be taken seriously. On the basis of its mention in the *Matsya* and other old Purāṇas, we can accept its existence, in some form or other, much prior to the Mohammadan invasions to the North. Jogesh Chandra Roy holds that the Purāṇa was composed during the 8th century A.D. The upper limit of the date of composition may tentatively be fixed in the 8th century because Śaṅkarācārya who flourished in the same century, is mentioned in the *Śrikṛṣṇajanmakhaṇḍa*.[18] It is also probable that by the tenth century, it began to be changed.[19]

Jayadeva, the Sanskrit poet, who flourished in the 12th century, was acquainted with the *Brahmavaivartapurāṇa*, the text of which was almost settled by that time.[20] The opening verse of Jayadeva's *Gitagovinda* (*Meghairmeduramambaram*, etc.) definitely alludes to an episode narrated in the 15th Chapter of the *Śrikṛṣṇajanmakhaṇḍa*. Jayadeva also describes Kṛṣṇa in his two aspects, *aiśvarya* and *mādhurya*, in the same line with *Brahmavaivarta*. It cannot, of course, be ruled out that interpolations, particularly of the *smṛti* material, continued till the 16th century or even till a little later. It can be safely presumed that the additions and alterations were carried out in Bengal. A close examination of the idiom and diction proves the fact beyond any reasonable doubt. The mixed castes like *Haḍḍi*, *Bāgatita*, etc. as mentioned in the Purāṇa, are found in no other part of the country than Bengal.[21] Gopālabhaṭṭa, one of the early Gosvāmīs of the Chaitanya sect, who flourished in the 16th century, found the *Brahmavaivarta-purāṇa*, almost in its present form, because, a little over sixty verses quoted by him in his *Haribhaktivilāsa*, from *Brahmavaivarta*, can be traced to that text.

It has already been mentioned that the extant *Brahmavaivartapurāṇa* comprises both ancient and medieval materials. It is difficult to ascertain the time of composition of ancient portions. Dr. Hazra is quite justified in his statement: "it seems highly probable that before 700 A.D. there existed a *Brahmavaivarta* which is now lost."[22]

— **Prof. Satkari Mukhopadhyaya**

NOTES

1. इतिहासपुराणाभ्यां वेदं समुपबृंहयेत्।
   बिभेत्यल्पश्रुताद्वेदो मामयं प्रहरेदिति॥ MBh. 1.1.260
2. II.4.10; IV.1.2; IV.5.11.
3. "पुराणम् 'असद्वा इदमग्र आसीत्' इत्यादीनि।" on. II.4.10
4. *op. cit.*
5. रथन्तरस्य कल्पस्य वृत्तान्तमधिकृत्य च।
   सावर्णिना नारदाय कृष्णमाहात्म्यमुत्तमम्॥
   यत्र ब्रह्मवराहस्य चरितं वर्ण्यते मुहुः।
   तदष्टादशसाहस्रं ब्रह्मवैवर्तमुच्यते॥

   —*Matsyapurāṇa*, Ch 53.
6. व्यासश्चतुर्धा संव्यस्य ब्रह्मवैवर्तसंज्ञितम्।
   तदष्टादशसाहस्रं पुराणं परिकीर्तितम्॥

   —*Nāradapurāṇa*, Ch 101.
7. तदष्टादशसाहस्रं ब्रह्मवैवर्तमीप्सितम्।

   —*Brahmavaivarta Purāṇa*, IV.133.16.
8. IV. 133.7.
9. सृष्टिश्चापि विसृष्टिश्च स्थितिस्तेषां च पालनम्।
   कर्मणां वासना वार्ता मनूनां चाग्रमेण च॥
   वर्णनं प्रलयानां च मोक्षस्य च निरूपणम्।
   तत्कीर्तनं हरेरेव वेदानां च पृथक् पृथक्॥

   —*Brahmavaivarta Purāṇa*, IV.133.8-9.
10. Hazra, R.C. *The Purāṇas in The Cultural Heritage of India*, Vol. II, 2nd edn., Ramakrishna Mission Institute of Culture, Calcutta, 1962, pp. 251-52.
11. प्रथमे वर्तते प्रश्च कृतिः स्यात् सृष्टिवाचकः।
    सृष्टेराद्या च या देवी प्रकृतिः सा प्रकीर्तिता॥

    —*Brahmavaivartapurāṇa*, II.1.8.

12. स्वेच्छामयस्येच्छया च श्रीकृष्णस्य सिसृक्षया।
साऽऽविर्बभूव सहसा मूलप्रकृतिरीश्वरी॥
तदिच्छया पञ्चविधा सृष्टिकर्मणि भेदतः।
अथ भक्तानुरोधाद्वा भक्तानुग्रहविग्रहा॥

—*Ibid.*, II.1.12-13.

13. गणेशजननी दुर्गा राधा लक्ष्मीः सरस्वती।
सावित्री वै सृष्टिविधौ प्रकृतिः पञ्चधा स्मृता॥

—*Ibid.*, II.1.1.

14. IV. 15. 120-130.

15. *loc.cit.*

16. Hazra, R.C., *Studies in Puranic records on Hindu Rites and Customs*, 2nd ed., MLBD, 1975, pp.166-167; *The Purāṇas, loc.cit.*

17. Wilson, H.H., *Essays*, Vol. 1, p. 120.

18. कारागारे च संसारे दुर्वहं निगडं परम्।
अच्छेद्यं ज्ञानखड्गैश्च महद्भिः शङ्करादिभिः॥

—*Brahmavaivarta Purāṇa, IV.* 24.18.

19. Hazra, R.C., *Studies in the Purāṇic records on Hindu Rites and Customs*, 2nd edn., MLBD, Delhi, 1975, pp.166-167.

20. De, Sushil Kumar, *Early history of the Vaishnava Faith and Movement in Bengal*, 2nd edn., Firma K.L. Mukhopadhyay, Calcutta, 1961, pp.11-12.

21. I.10.105, 118.

22. *Studies in the Purāṇic records on Hindu Rites and Customs*, p.167.

BRAHMAVAIVARTA PURĀṆA

BRAHMA KHAṆḌA

Invocation

1. Obeisance to that Supreme Lord always worshipped by (the gods) Gaṇeśa (Lord of the *gaṇas*, a class of semi-divine beings), Brahmā, Īṣa (Lord Śiva), Sureśa (Indra, the lord of the celestials), Śeṣa (the serpent-god), the celestials, the Manus (the different rulers of the earth), the eminent saints and the goddesses such as Sarasvatī (goddess of learning; the consort of Lord Brahmā), Śrī (goddess of wealth; the consort of Lord Viṣṇu) and Girijā (mountain-born, denoting Pārvatī, the consort of Lord Śiva).

2. I adore in (my) heart that unborn, great, eternal first principle intent on creation that brought forth the gross bodies, the three qualities, the first being and the universe in the pores of the skin and then created the subtle things by means of his power.

3. I contemplate with devotion that embodiment of self-will that transcends the three qualities, changeless and desireless, and that which assumes a dark form (as Kṛṣṇa) having incomparable beauty, for the sole purpose of contemplation and that which the celestials, men, Manus and yogins, deep-rooted in yoga, contemplate and that which pious men after several births and by doing penance are not able to perceive even in their dreams.

4. I adore that undecaying Supreme Brahman, Lord Kṛṣṇa, transcending the qualities, from whom have sprung up the nature (the original source of the material world), Brahmā, Viṣṇu and Śiva.

Om! Obeisance to Lord Vāsudeva (Lord Kṛṣṇa, son of Vasudeva)!

INTRODUCTORY

1. After having saluted Lord Nara-Nārāyaṇa*, the foremost man, goddess Sarasvatī and (the sage) Vyāsa, one should narrate the Jaya.**

2. The revered (sage) Vyāsa milked the celestial cow goddess Sarasvatī, the wonderful embodiment of nectar, having the collection of *vedas* as the calf. O infatuated ones! You all repeatedly drink the inexhaustible and favourite milk, this extremely sweet Brahmavaivarta *purāṇa.*

CHAPTER ONE

Contents of the Purāṇa

1. The sages Śaunaka and others in the Naimiṣa forest in Bhārata were seated on the *kuśa* (grass) after having performed the daily and obligatory rites.

2. In the meanwhile they beheld a bard coming there and modestly bowing to them. They offered him a seat.

3. The tranquil (sage) Śaunaka, the foremost among the sages, honoured the guest, the tranquil knower of the *purāṇas,* and enquired him with pleasure about his welfare.

4-8. The delighted (Śaunaka) asked the smiling and modest (bard), the knower of all the principles and the *Purāṇas,* after relieving him of the fatigue of his journey, and providing him a comfortable seat. As he was shining in the midst of the assembly of sages like the moon among the stars in the sky (Śaunaka asked him) about the excellent *Purāṇa* containing the episode relating to Kṛṣṇa that was pleasing to the ears, auspicious, deserving felicity, conferring

---

* Denotes Kṛṣṇa, originally regarded as identical, but in later literature considered as distinct, Nara denoting Arjuna and Nārāyaṇa denoting Kṛṣṇa.

** the fundamental meaning of the word is victory. But it denotes the Mahābhārata in one of its stages of growth. Vyāsa is traditionally believed to be the author of the Mahābhārata and the Purāṇas.

auspiciousness, repository of auspiciousness, the seed of all auspiciousness always bringing forth prosperity destroying all inauspiciousness, the excellent one conferring all prosperity, yielding devotion to Lord Hari, giving always happiness, bestowing beatitude from mundane existence, imparting knowledge about the principles (or truth) and makes the wives, children and grandchildren flourish.

Śaunaka said:

9-10. Where do you propose to go and wherefrom do you come? Prosperity unto you. What an auspicious day it is for us today that we have seen you. We alone are afraid of *kaliyuga* bereft of qualifying knowledge. Although we are desirous of beatitude we are drowned in mundane existence. (It seems) that you have come here for that purpose.

11. You are well-versed in the *purāṇas* (and hence referred to as) knower of *purāṇas*. You are conversant with all the *purāṇas* and are extremely kind.

12-14. O ! Fortunate one ! You narrate me that *purāṇa* which increases one's knowledge engendering steady and permanent devotion towards Śrī Kṛṣṇa. (That devotion) is even greater than (beatitude). It cuts at the root of fate. It cuts asunder the fetters of those bound by mundane existence. It showers a rain of nectar for those consumed by the conflagration of temporal existence. O Bard ! It always gives happiness and delight to the hearts of beings.

15. It is verily the seed of all (things) and it proves (the existence of) the Supreme Brahman. It is glorified as superior to the creation made by that Supreme Brahman ever bent on creation.

16. (Kindly enlighten me) about that Brahman, endowed with a form and without a form and is of the form of the Supreme Soul. What is its form and how is it to be contemplated ?

17. Whom do the devotees of Lord Viṣṇu and tranquil ascetics contemplate ? (Describe me) the chief import of that subtle one enunciated in the *vedas.*

18. (Enlighten me) about that, that is of the form of the primordial thing and in which the beings have been proved to lie and that in which are determined the characteristics of the qualities and the principles such as the *mahat* (the great principle according to Sāṅkhya).

19. (Narrate me) that which contains descriptions of the Goloka (world of cows), the Vaikuṇṭha (the abode of Lord Viṣṇu), the Śivaloka (the abode of Lord Śiva) and the heaven.

20. O Sauti ! (Describe me) (that) which explains the part-manifestations and parts (of the Lord). What are the modifications of the Primordial Being? What is the *prakṛti* (Primordial Being)? What is the soul higher than the *prakṛti*?

21. (Narrate me) that which contains (the description of) the secret birth of the celestials and the celestial women, the origin of the oceans, mountains and rivers.

22. What are the part (manifestations)? What are the parts of *prakṛti* ? What are the part and partless ? (Describe us) their life histories, contemplation, worship, glorification and the like which are auspicious.

23. (Narrate me that) which describes (the goddesses) Durgā (consort of Lord Śiva), Sarasvatī (consort of Lord Brahmā), Lakṣmī (consort of Lord Viṣṇu) and Sāvitri (consort of Sun-god) and wherein we find the rare, nectar-like legends of Rādhā (cowherdess companion of Lord Kṛṣṇa).

24. (Expound me that) which describes the fruits of actions of the beings, the hells, the criticism of actions and the means of liberation from them.

25-26. Elucidate me the different good and bad positions (attained) by the beings, the different kinds of births (gained) by the beings (on account) of their actions, the different diseases that are the outcome of the actions of beings and the means of gaining release from the actions.

27. (Describe me) that which deals with the auspicious legends of (goddesses) Manasā (a daughter of sage Kaśyapa), Tulasī (Holy Basil personified), Kāli (a form of consort of Śiva), Gaṅgā (the river Ganges), Pṛthvi (earth) and Vasundharā (earth) (supporting beings) and others.

28. (Describe me) that which deals with the *śālagrāma* [1] stones and about gifts. O Sauti ! (Describe me) that (*purāṇa*) which expounds the virtuous acts and sinful acts.

29. (Narrate me) that which contains the legends of Gaṇeśvara (Lord of semi-divine beings), his birth and acts, and that which describes the secret amulets, hymns and mystic formulae.

30. Bearing in mind all the most wonderful legends which are rare and not heard before you are competent to describe me now.

31-37. You are competent to describe me that which contains (an account of) Lord Kṛṣṇa, the Supreme Soul, such as his birth and wandering in the holy land of Bhārata and the world. O Sage ! In which holy house of a holy person he was born? Which fortunate, chaste, meritorious and respectable lady gave birth to that son ? After his manifestation in that house where did he proceed and what for ? After going there what did he do and how did he return ? By whom he was beseeched to manifest (and relieve oppression on the earth) and (why) did he graze the cows ? Why did he lay the bridge and come to Goloka (the cowherd colony) again ? You are the proper person to explain me this and such other legends, the *purāṇa* that is difficult to be heard, difficult to be known by the sages, that is the cause of purification of the mind, that is good or bad which I have asked or not asked according to the range of my knowledge and that which at once produces indifference to worldly things. One who explains that which a disciple has asked or not asked is said to be a noble preceptor, most excellent among the pious and treats alike the worthy and unworthy.

38. Sauti said: I am in good health because of the sight of your lotus feet. I have come from the holy place of the *siddhas* (accomplished persons) and I am proceeding to the hermitage of Nārāyaṇa (Lord Viṣṇu).

39. I have come here to see the assembly of brahmins, convey my obeisance and to see the Naimiṣa forest, that yields merit in Bhārata.

40. Out of ignorance if one does not make obeisance to the Lord, a brahmin and the preceptor, he gets caught in the thread of time as long as the Sun and Moon last.

41. Lord Hari (Viṣṇu) treads over the earth in the form of a brahmin. A virtuous one should bow to a brahmin, a form of Lord Hari, out of merit.

42. O Noble Sir ! Whatever has been asked by you, everything that is desired has been known. The excellent Brahmavaivarta is the essence among all the *purāṇas.*

43. It dispels the delusion of the other *purāṇas* and *vedas.* It yields devotion to Lord Hari. It promotes all knowledge of realities.

44. This yields the desires of the seekers. It confers emancipation on those that seek. It bestows devotion for the *vaiṣṇavas* (devotees of Lord Viṣṇu). It is of the form of a wish-yielding tree.

45. (The section) Brahma Khaṇḍa is the seed of everything and establishes the Supreme Brahman, whom the pious ascetics and devotees of Viṣṇu meditate.

46. O Saunaka ! The devotees of Viṣṇu, ascetics and pious men are not different. By the gradual transformation of their ignorance they become different beings by stages.

47. They become virtuous by association with the virtuous and ascetics by their contact with the ascetics. The devotees of Viṣṇu become gradually pious ascetics on account of their association with the devotees.

48. In which there is (a description) of the origin of gods, goddesses and all beings that Prakṛti Khaṇḍa (describes) the auspicious legends of the goddesses.

49. (It describes) the fruits of the deeds of beings and deals with the *śālagrāma*[2], their amulets, hymns, sacred formulae and worship.

50. It also describes the characteristic of *prakṛti* and the parts of the *kalās.* There is proclamation of their glories and their greatness.

51. The descriptions of the auspicious and inauspicious destinations of good and bad people, the hells, diseases and the release therefrom (are found herein).

52. Then in (the section) Gaṇeśa Khaṇḍa it describes the origin of that (Lord). That legend is very rare and very difficult (to be found) in the *vedas.*

53. The real nature of things are described in the dialogue between Gaṇeśa and sage Bhṛgu. It then deals with the secret amulet, hymn, mystic formulae and tantra (ritualistic procedures).

54-55. The section dealing with the birth of (Lord) Kṛṣṇa is glorified to be the next one. The birth of Lord Kṛṣṇa in the sacred place in Bhārata, his deeds, the removal of oppression on earth, the auspicious and wonderful sports and the laying of the bridge for the pious have been dealt with in the section describing (his) birth.

56. O Brahmin ! This most excellent *purāṇa* in four sections dealing with all virtuous acts has been narrated.

57. This *purāṇa* known as the Brahmavaivarta is capable of conferring prosperity sought by all. It is the cause of fulfilment of all desires and is capable of bestowing all the desired fruits.

58. This forms the essence of all the Purāṇas and is entirely connected with the *vedas.* O Śaunaka ! Brahman in its entirety has been explained by (Lord) Kṛṣṇa here.

59-60. Those well-versed in ancient lore hence call it the Brahmavaivarta. This string of *purāṇas* has been given by (Lord) Kṛṣṇa, the Supreme Being, to Brahmā in the world of cows free from disease in days of yore. (Lord) Brahmā gave it to Dharma (embodiment of virtue) in the great holy place Puṣkara[3].

61. It was given gladly to his son Nārāyaṇa by Dharma[4]. Nārāyaṇa imparted to it (sage) Nārada.

62-63. (Sage) Nārada delivered it to Vyāsadeva on the banks of Jāhnavi (daughter of sage Jahnu; denotes river Ganges). Vyāsa divided this extensive string of *purāṇas* and gave it to me in the beautiful, meritorious and *siddhakṣetra* (a place that accomplishes one's efforts). O Brahmin ! I have narrated this to you . You listen to that in full .

64. This *purāṇa* expounded by Vyāsa (contains) eighteen thousand (verses). The fruit that one gets by listening to the whole of the *purāṇa,* would certainly be got by listening to this chapter.

CHAPTER TWO

Exposition about the Supreme Brahman

Śaunaka said :

1. O Sauti ! What is that rare (exposition) you have heard? Narrate me in detail that most wonderful and unsurpassing Brahma Khaṇḍa, that is dear.

Sauti said :

2-3. I make obeisance to the lotus feet of the most radiant preceptor Vyāsa. After making obeisance to (Lord) Hari, the celestials and the Brahmins, I expound the perpetual virtues, the unsurpassing Brahma Khaṇḍa, which I have heard from Vyāsa. It dispels the darkness of ignorance and illuminates the path of knowledge.

4. O Brahmin! In days of yore there was only a cluster of light resembling multitudes of Suns, everlasting, immeasurable and the cause of the universe at the time of the deluge.

5. That light of the Lord, an embodiment of self-will was much radiant. The three worlds inside that light were charming.

6-9. O Brahmin ! The world of the cows was above that eternal like the lord. It was circular in shape extending to three crores of *yojanas*[1]. It was lustrous, wide, excellent and was verily a jewel-ground. It was imperceptible. It could be perceived by the ascetics in their dreams and attained by the devotees of (Lord) Viṣṇu. As it remained in the inter-region (between the heaven and earth) it was supported by the Lord by means of yoga. It was devoid of calamities, diseases, old age, death, grief and fear. It was made beautiful by countless shrines adorned by gems. At the time of dissolution it is in the company of (Lord) Kṛṣṇa. It is surrounded by the cowherds and cowherdesses at the time of creation.

10. The Vaikuṇṭha (abode of Viṣṇu) and Śivaloka (abode of Śiva) are situated below on the right and left extending to fifty crores *yojanas* and equally charming.

11. The Vaikuṇṭha, circular in shape, extending to a crore of *yojanas*, is void at the time of deluge and is endowed with (Lord) Lakṣmīnārāyaṇa (Lord Viṣṇu together with his consort Lakṣmī) at the time of creation.

12. The Lord endowed with four arms is in the company of the assembly of men, devoid of old age, death etc. The world of Śiva on the left is a crore *yojanas* extensive.

13-14. It is void at deluge and is in the company of Śiva and His attendants at (the time of) creation. Inside the cow-world (there is) an extremely charming lustre. It causes much delight. It always makes (people) much happy. The ascetics always meditate it by means of *yoga* with eyes of wisdom.

15. That is the cause of delight. It is without any form. It is the most supreme. There is an extremely beautiful form within that lustre.

16. (That form) is dark (in colour) like that of a fresh cloud. It has red lotus-like eyes. That form is adorned with a spotless face resembling the autumnal moon.

17. It has the beauty of a crore of god of love. It is the abode of divine sport. It is delightful. It possesses two arms. It holds the flute in the hand. It is smiling. It wears an yellow garment.

18. It is adorned with manifold most excellent ornaments. It is kind to devotees. It is besmeared with sandal all over its

limbs. It is endowed with musk and saffron.

19. Its chest is marked with a curl of hair. It is adorned with the shining *kaustubha* (a celebrated gem). It is radiant with the crown set with excellent gems.

20. It is seated on a gemmed lotus seat and is adorned with a garland of wild flowers. It is the Supreme Brahman. It is glorious and eternal.

21. It is an embodiment of self-will. It is the seed of all (things). It is the support of everything. It is the most supreme. It is young. It is always clad in the dress of a cowherd.

22. It is endowed with the beauty of a crore of full-moons. It confers grace on its devotees. It has no desire, (and it is) changeless. It is perfectly complete. It is the Lord.

23. It is at the centre of the circle of (dancing) cowherdesses. It is tranquil. It is the excellent Lord of dance. It is auspicious, worthy of auspiciousness and conferer of auspiciousness.

24. It is the seed of supreme happiness. It is true, imperishable and incorruptible. It holds sway over all accomplishments. It is of the forms of all accomplishments. It bestows all accomplishments.

25. It is superior to *prakṛti*. It is the presiding Lord, devoid of qualities and an embodiment of eternity. It is the first being, unmanifest, invoked by many and glorified by many.

26. It is true, independent and it is of the form of the Supreme Soul. The devotees of (Lord) Viṣṇu meditate that tranquil and supreme path.

27. That fortunate one bearing such a form is the only one. He beheld (before creation) the entire universe together with the different quarters and the sky as void.

CHAPTER THREE

The Exposition about Creation

Sauti said :

1-3. O Brahmin ! Beholding the universe entirely void and the cow-world dreadful without habitation, without water, without wind, enveloped by darkness, devoid of trees, mountains, modifications, crops, grass etc., the Lord, an embodiment of self-will, mentally began His creation of all beings out of His self-will and unaided.

4. At the beginning of creation, the three qualities which are the cause of human existence and are embodied, manifested on His right side.

5. Then (manifested) (the principles) known as *mahat* (great), ego, the five subtle principles, form, taste, smell, touch and sound.

6-9. After that manifested the Lord Nārāyaṇa Himself. He was a dark-complexioned youth. He was clad in yellow garment. He was wearing a garland of wild flowers. He had four arms. He was holding the conch, disc, mace and lotus. He was having a smiling lotus face. He was adorned with gemmed ornaments. He was holding a bow. He was adorned with the *kaustubha* (gem) and bearing the curl of hair on the chest. He is the abode of goddess of wealth. He is the treasure-house of prosperity.[1]

He is the source of ascertaining prosperity. He is charming with the moon-like face besmeared with the radiance of the autumnal moon. He is beautiful with a graceful form endowed with the lustre of god of love. He stood in front of Lord Kṛṣṇa and glorified Him with folded palms.

Nārāyaṇa said :

10-13. I make obeisance (to you), the excellent and the most desirable. (You are) the conferer of boons. (You are) worthy of excellence. (You are) the cause of boons, the cause of causes, actions and the cause of those actions. (You are)the penance, the perennial bestower of the fruits of penance, the Lord of penance and the doer of penances. (You are) black like the fresh clouds. (You are) delighted in your own self. (You are)beautiful. (You are) desireless and of the form of desire. (You are) the destroyer of desire and the cause of desire. (You are) everything and the Lord of all things. (You are) of the form of the seed of everything and are outstanding. (You are)of the form of the *vedas.* (You had) the origin from the *vedas.* (You are) the conferer of the fruits described in the *vedas.* (You are) the fruits. (You are) the knower of the *vedas* and their application. (You are) outstanding among all the knowers of the *vedas.*

14. After having spoken thus with devotion, He sat on the charming gem-studded throne in front of that Supreme person, being commanded by Him.

15. Whoever reads this hymn uttered by (Lord) Nārāyaṇa daily in the three twilights with a composed mind, that person never incurs a sin.

16. The seeker of progeny gains the offspring. One that desires to get a wife gets the dear one. One that had lost his kingdom gains the kingdom. One that had lost his wealth gains wealth.

17. One that has been imprisoned and seized by calamities becomes free by this hymn. One that is sick gets rid of his sickness after listening to this hymn with devotion.

Sauti said :

18. Thereafter manifested from his left side a rude form possessing the hue of pure crystal and having five faces.

19. That outstanding one was bearing a matted hair having the colour of heated gold. He had a gently smiling pleasant face having three eyes and the crescent on the head.

20. He was holding the trident, a sharp-edged spear and the rosary. He was the Lord of all accomplishments. He was an accomplished one. He was the preceptor of the preceptors of most excellent ascetics.

21. He was the Destroyer of the God of Death. He was Lord Śiva, the Destroyer and Conqueror of Death. He was the bliss of wisdom. He was a great knower. He was the supreme bestower of great knowledge.

22. His face possessing the lustre of the full-moon was delightful to behold. He was the foremost among the devotees of (Lord) Viṣṇu. He was glowing with the lustre of brahman (Supreme Being).

23. Standing in front of Lord Kṛṣṇa, he eulogised him with folded hands with horripilation on all the limbs, tears swelling in the eyes and extremely faltering tone.

*Mahādeva said :**

24. "I make my obeisance to the form of victory, conferrer of success, Lord of conquest, the cause of victory and the foremost among the bestowers of victory and the invincible.

25. (You are) the universe. (You are) the Lord of the Lord, cause and support of the universe. (You are) the embodiment of the universe. (You are) the cause of the cause of universe.

26. You are the cause of the protection of the universe. (You are) the destroyer of the universe. (You are) the outstanding among those having the universe as the source. (You are) the seed and support of the fruits. (You are) the fruit. (You are) the conferrer of that fruit.

27. (You are) of the form of lustre, conferrer of lustre and most excellent among those having radiance." After having spoken thus and making obeisance to (Lord) Nārāyaṇa and after conversing, He sat on an excellent gem-studded throne being commanded by Him.

28. Whoever reads with self-control this hymn uttered by (Lord) Śambhu (Śiva), he accomplishes everything and gains victory at every step.

29-33. His friends, wealth and prosperity always increase. The army of his enemies, grief and calamities get destroyed. Thus ends the hymn on Lord Kṛṣṇa spoken (by) Lord Śambhu in the Brahmavaivarta (Purāṇa).

Sauti said :

"Then manifested from the navel lotus of (Lord) Kṛṣṇa, a great ascetic. He was infirm and holding a kamaṇḍalu (a kettle-shaped small vessel for religious purposes). He was excellent. He was wearing a white apparel. He had white teeth and white hair. He had four faces. He is the master of yogins. He is the Lord of craftsmen. He is the father of all (beings). He is the preceptor. He is the bestower of the fruits of penaṇce. He is the conferer of all prosperities. He is the creator, ordainer, maker and dispensor of all acts. He is the Dispenser of the four *vedas.* He is the knower. He is the Lord that delivers the *vedas.* He is tranquil. He is the consort of (goddess) Sarasvatī. He has a good conduct. He is the abode of compassion."

34. Standing in front of Śrī Kṛṣṇa, he extolled Him with folded palms with horripilation on all his limbs and having bent-neck on account of devotion.

Brahmā said:

35-37. I salute Lord Kṛṣṇa, the cowherd that transcends the qualities, the undecaying, unmanifest, immutable and manifest. He is clad in the dress of a cowherd. He is young and tranquil. He is the beautiful favourite of the cowherdesses. He has a dark complexion resembling a fresh rain-bearing cloud. He has the beauty of manifold gods of love. He is stationed in the circle of sportive dance in the vicinity of the forest of Vṛndāvana. He is the master of sportive dance. He stays in the sportive dance. He is extremely desirous of delighting dances.

38. After having spoken thus and bowing down he sat on the excellent gem-studded throne at his command after having conversed with (Lords) Nārāyaṇa (Viṣṇu) and Īśa (Śiva).

39. Whoever reads this hymn sung by (Lord) Brahmā after waking up in the morning, all his sins would get destroyed and bad dreams would become good.

40. (For such a person) there would be devotion towards Govinda (the cowherd). It would increase (the number of) sons and grandsons. Infancy would get destroyed. His glorious fame would ever increase.

41. Thus ends the hymn sung by (Lord) Brahmā in the Brahmavaivarta (Purāṇa).

Sauti said :

"Then there manifested a smiling person from the chest of the Supreme Soul. He had a white complexion. He had a matted hair.

42-43. He is (Lord) Dharma, the witness of everything, omniscient of all the acts of all (the beings). He is impartial everywhere. He is compassionate. He is non-injurious and devoid of wrath. He is endowed with the knowledge of righteousness. He is rooted in piety. He confers righteousness. He alone is the virtue of the virtuous. He is the Supreme Soul. He is the product of the fruits.

44. Standing in front of Śrī Kṛṣṇa and making prostration, he eulogised the Supreme god, the Lord of all beings and the bestower of all things."

Śri Dharma said :

45-47. "(Obeisance to) (Lord) Kṛṣṇa, (Lord) Viṣṇu, (Lord) Vāsudeva (Son of Vasudeva), the Supreme Soul, the Lord, the cowherd, the Supreme Bliss, the single undecaying and unmutilating, the Lord of the cowherds, the Lord of the cowherdesses, the cowherd, the protector of the cows, the sovereign, the Lord of the cows, One that dwells in the cow-shed, One that holds the tail of the calf, One that is stationed in the midst of the cows, cowherds and cowherdesses, the Principal one, and the Foremost person."

48. After having spoken thus and standing up he conversed with (Lords) Brahmā, Viṣṇu and Maheśa and sat on the excellent gem-studded throne.

49. Whoever reads these twenty-four names issued forth from the mouths of Dharma, after getting up in the morning, he would always be happy and victorious.

50. At the time of his death, the name of (Lord) Hari would certainly accrue to him. He attains the place of (Lord) Hari at the end. He would certainly get (the vision of) the face of (Lord) Hari.

51. Virtuous (events) would occur to him everyday and he would not be inclined to do unrighteous acts. The benefits of the four-fold goals could always accrue to him.

52. Similar to the serpents (running away on seeing) Vainsteya (son of Vinatā, the vehicle of Lord Viṣṇu), all fears, grief and sins run away out of fear on seeing him.

53-57. Thus ends the hymn on Śrī Kṛṣṇa made by Dharma in the Brahmavaivarta (Purāṇa).

Sauti said :

"There manifested a girl from the left side of Dharma. She had such a form as if she was a second lotus-based (Goddess Lakṣmī). Then manifested a goddess from the face of the Supreme Lord. She had white complexion and was holding the lute and a book. She had the lustre of manifold full-moons. Her eyes resembled the lotus of the autumn. She wore an apparel pure like the fire. She was adorned with gemmed ornaments. She was smiling. She had beautiful teeth. She was elegant. She was most beautiful among the beautiful. She is the outstanding mother of the scriptures, treatises and learned (people). She is the presiding deity of speech. She is the favourite deity of the poets. She is of the form of pure goodness. She is tranquil (goddess) Sarasvatī.

58-59. She stood in front of Govinda(Kṛṣṇa). At first she sang the glory of His name and fame on the lute and then danced. She extolled with folded palms all the deeds of Lord Hari performed in different *kalpa*[2] (periods) and *yuga*[3] (periods).

Sarasvatī said :

60-63. "I salute (that person) in the midst of the dancing circle, desirous of delighting in dancing, seated on a gem-studded throne and adorned with gem-studded ornaments. He is the master of dancing. He is dance-maker. He is the master of danseuse. He is the presiding Lord of dancing. He amuses himself in dancing. He gets exhausted with fatigue due to dancing. He sports in dancing. He is the beloved of the cowherdesses desirous of dancing. He is tranquil and handsome." After having extolled thus and bowing down she sat contented on an excellent gem-studded throne with a smiling face.

64. Whoever reads this hymn made by goddess Vāṇī (Sarasvatī) after getting up in the morning, he would always become wise, wealthy, learned and blessed with progeny.

65. Thus ends the hymn on (Lord) Kṛṣṇa made by (goddess) Sarasvatī in the Brahmavaivarta (Purāṇa).

Sauti said :

Then there manifested from the mind of (Lord) Kṛṣṇa a goddess having white complexion and adorned with gem-studded ornament.

66. She was wearing a yellow garment. She was young and smiling. She presides over all prosperity. She is the conferer of all wealth. She is the goddess of heaven in the heaven. She is the goddess of the kingdom in kings.

67. She stood in front of (Lord) Hari and extolled the Supreme Soul and master after bowing to Him with bent neck out of devotion.

Mahālakṣmī said :

68. "I make obeisance to the form of truth, the master of truth, the seed of truth and the perpetual one. He is the support of truth. He knows truth. He is the source of truth."

69-70. After having spoken thus and bowing down she sat on a comfortable seat. Then manifested (a goddess) from the intellect of Supreme Soul having the hue of heated gold and illuminating the directions with her radiance. She is the presiding deity of all (the beings). She is the *mūlaprakṛti* (nature). She is the governess.

71. She has the hue of heated gold. She has the lustre of manifold *suns.* She has a gently smiling and pleasing face. She possesses eyes resembling the lotus of the autumn.

72-73. She is clad in red dress. She is adorned with gem-studded ornament. She is the governing deity of all the energies relating to sleep, desire, hunger, thirst, compassion, earnestness and forbearance. She is frightful. She is (goddess) Durga having hundred arms. She destroys evil propensities and afflictions.

74-76. She is the form of energy of the soul. She is the supreme mother of the world. She holds the trident, spear, bow (of Viṣṇu), bow, sword and arrows, conch, disc, mace, rosary, *kamaṇḍalu* (small vessel carried by ascetics), thunderbolt, goad, noose, *bhuśuṇḍī* (a sort of missile), stick, an iron club, the weapons known as Nārāyaṇa, Brahmā, Rudra, Pāśupata, Parjanya, Varuṇa, Vahni and Gandharva. She stood in front of (Lord) Kṛṣṇa and extolled Him with rejoice.

Prakṛti said :

77. I am *prakṛti.* I am the governess ruling over all beings. I am the form of all beings. I am the form of all energies. This world derives its energy from me.

78-79. I have been created by you. I am not independent. You are the Lord of the world. You are the refuge, protector, creator and destroyer. You are the ordainer. You are the creator in order to create. You are the destroyer in order to destroy. You are the ordainer that lays down. With pleasure I bow to you, the form of Supreme Bliss. Brahmā would fall down at the winking time of the eye (brow).

80-81. O Lord! Who has the ability to describe the imcomparable greatness ? You would create multitudes of

Viṣṇus, the movable and immovable beings in the Universe and the celestials beginning with Brahmā, merely by the sportive winking of the eye-brow. How many goddesses like me indeed you are capable of creating sportively !

82. "I salute with rejoice that Being of fullness, worthy of adoration. O Lord! I make obeisance with pleasure to that Supreme Soul, the Lord, of whom the great first Being is a part and which is the basis of the manifold forms of the Universe.

83. I salute that Being that is greater than *prakṛti* whom (Lords) Brahmā, Viṣṇu, Śiva and others the *vedas,* and Vāṇī (Sarasvatī) cannot extol.

84. The *vedas* and (men) outstanding among the learned, capable of eulogising, are not able (to extol). One that is beyond aiming, who can extol? I bow to that desireless being."

85. After having spoken thus that (goddess) Durgā sat on an excellent gem-studded throne. The celestials bowed to Śrī Kṛṣṇa and extolled her.

86. Whoever reads this hymn on the Supreme Being (Lord) Kṛṣṇa made by goddess Durgā at the time of offering worship would be victorious and have all round happiness.

87. (Goddess) Durgā would never go away abandoning his house any time. He would be radiant with his glory in the ocean of mundane existence. He would finally attain the place of Śrī Hari.

CHAPTER FOUR

Manifestation of Minor Gods

Sauti said :

1. "Then manifested from the tip of the tongue of (Lord) Kṛṣṇa, a goddess, beautiful and having the complexion of pure crystal.

2. She was wearing a white dress and adorned with all ornaments. She was holding a rosary. She was known as (goddess) Sāvitrī.

3. That pious one stood in front of the Supreme Brahman, the eternal being, and extolled him with her folded palms and neck bent on account of devotion.

Sāvitrī said :

4. "I salute you, the seed of everything. You are eternal and radiant brahman. You are greater than the great. You have a dark complexion . You are changeless and unstained."

5. After having spoken thus that smiling goddess sat on excellent throne after bowing to Śrī Hari once again delivering the scriptures.

6. Then manifested a male being resembling the colour of heated gold, from the mind of (Lord) Kṛṣṇa, the Supreme Being.

7. He agitates the minds of all lustful persons with his five shafts. Hence men called him by the name 'Manmatha' (god of love).

8. Then came into being the excellent spouse of the god of love from the left side of that man. She was extremely graceful and was captivating all.

9. She was the delight of all. Hence beholding that smiling good woman, men call her by the name 'Rati'.

10. After glorifying (Lord) Hari in her company, he (Manmatha) sat on a gem-studded throne in front of (Lord) Hari. He had five shafts. He was wielding a bow.

11. He wields the five shafts — killing, stupefying, soporific, emaciating and maddening.[1]

12. God of love threw all the shafts in order to test them. Then all became lustful on account of the will of god.

13. Beholding Rati, the seed of Brahmā fell. Becoming ashamed, the great meditator stood there covering with a cloth.

14. Then there arose the Fire-god after burning the cloth. He had a magnitude of manifold palms. He was possessing glowing flames.

15. Beholding that it is growing, (Lord) Kṛṣṇa sportively created water together with the exhaling breath, ejecting a drop from the mouth.

16. O Brahmin! The drop of water from the mouth inundated the whole world. A drop of that water extinguished the fire.

17. Hence then onwards the fire gets extinguished by water. Then there manifested a male being that was the presiding deity of that (water).

18. There arose a male being from the water. He is known to be Varuṇa. He is the presiding deity of water. He is the master of all sea-monsters.

19. Then there manifested a maiden on the left side of that fire. Men refer to her as *svāhā,* the consort of Fire.

20. Then there came into being a maiden from the left side of the Lord of water (Varuṇa). She was known to be Varuṇāni, the beloved consort of Varuṇa.

21. Lord Wind came into being from the exhaling breath of the Lord (Kṛṣṇa). He is the life-breath of all the beings. The exhaling breath is its outcome.

22. Then there appeared a maiden from the left side of the Wind. She was the consort of Wind proclaimed as goddess Vāyavī.

23. (Then by the discharge) of the *kāmabāṇa* (weapon)of Kṛṣṇa, there was a fall of the semen. Being ashamed he purged it in the water in the presence of the celestials.

24. At the end of thousand years it attained the form of an egg. Then the great first Being came into being. He is the support of the universal flood.

25. The universe rests on one of his pores. He is grosser than the gross. He is great. There is no one superior to him.

26. He is a sixteenth part of (Lord) Kṛṣna, the Supreme Being. He is known to be (Lord) Mahāviṣṇu. He is the support of all. He is perpetual.

27. When he was reclining on the great ocean, just like the lotus leaf on water, there arose the two demons[2] originating from the impurity of the ears.

28. Rising up from the water they were intent on killing (Lord) Brahmā. Lord Nārāyaṇa killed them (by striking)at their loins.

29. Then the entire earth (was covered) by their entire fat. All the universe and the goddess Vasundhara are therein.

CHAPTER FIVE

The Periods of Time and the Creation of Goloka and Rādhā

Śaunaka said :

1. "Are the cows, cowherds and cowherdesses permanent in the Goloka? Or whether they are created ? You are fit to explain me for clearing my doubts.

Sauti said :

2. They are all created at the first creation. They remain through the subsequent deluges. O Brahmin! I have already described you the process of first creation.

3. At the time of the first creation (Lords) Nārāyaṇa and Maheśvara originate. They two as well as *prakṛti* remain manifest at the time of every deluge.

4. O Brahmin! I have described you the crea -tion relating to *Brahmakalpa*. You listen to my narration (relating to)the two kalpas — Varāha and Padma.

5. O sage! The kalpas are — three kinds of Brahma, Varāha and Padma– in the same way as there are four *yugas* duly described.

6. *Satya, tretā, dvāpara* and *kali* are the four yugas. One *divyayuga* is stated to be 360 yugas.

7. A *manvantara* consists of 71 Divyayugas. A day of Brahmā consists of the periods of 14 Manus.

8. A year of Brahmā consists of 360 days (of Brahmā). The life-span of Brahmā is stated to be 108 years.

9. This is the period of *nimeṣa* (winking of the eyebrow) of (Lord) Kṛṣṇa, the Supreme Being. Those who are conversant with (counting of) time have reckoned a *kalpa* with the life of Brahmā.

10. There are many kinds of minor kalpas known as *samvarta* and others. (Sage) Mārkaṇḍeya is stated to be living till the end of seven such *kalpa* periods.

11. That *kalpa* is reckoned by a single day of Brahmā. The life span of that sage(Mārkaṇḍeya) is said to be 7 days of (the life of) Brahmā.

12. Brahma, Varāha and Padma are the three *kalpas.* You listen to my narration of creation during the three kalpa periods.

13. After having created the earth in the Brahma (*kalpa*) the creator has made his creation with the fat of Madhu and Kaiṭabha at the command of the Lord.

14-15. Lifting with supreme effort the lost and drowned earth from the nether world by means of (Lord) Viṣṇu in the form of a boar in the Varāha (*kalpa*), the creator made the creation of the three worlds upto the Brahmaloka except the three eternal worlds in the navel lotus of (Lord) Viṣṇu in the Padma (*kalpa*).

16. I have described you the reckoning of time in explaining (the process of) creation. I have described you a little about creation. What more would you like to listen to ?

Śaunaka said :

17. What then did the glorious Lord of the *sāttvatas* do? You are fit to explain me what he did after creating them.

Sauti said:

18. Then after their creation, the great Lord and master of the Goloka, resorted to the charming circle of dance at the Goloka. The Lord was very attractive in their company.

19. In the midst of beautiful wish-yielding trees it was very captivating. It was a wide, even and smooth circle.

20. It was consecrated with sandal, *agallochum*, musk and saffron. It was flooded with curd, fried grain, flour, grain; *dūrvā* (grass) and leaves.

21. It was endowed with cloth and knotted thread. It was surrounded by collection of plantain (trees) and pillars decorated with fresh sandal (paste) and sprouts.

22-23. It was encircled by three crores of pavilions built with quality gems, illuminated by gemmed lamps and made fragrant with flowers and scented fumes. It was surrounded by collection of materials of enjoyment appropriate for decoration. It was adorned with bedsteads made elegant.

24. The Lord of the world went there and dwelt with them. O foremost sage ! They were surprised to behold the circle of dance.

25. There manifested a maiden from the left side of (Lord) Kṛṣṇa. She ran and brought flowers and offered arghya[1] at the feet of the Lord.

26. O foremost among brahmins ! As she had her origin in the dancing place at Goloka and was placed in front of (Lord) Hari, she was proclaimed as Rādhā by those conversant with the past.

27. She was the presiding deity of the life of (Lord) Kṛṣṇa, the Supreme Being. As she manifested from the life (of Lord Kṛṣṇa), she was dearer to Him than His life.

28. That goddess was aged 16 years and was endowed with maidenhood. She was wearing a dress as pure as the fire. She was smiling and attractive.

29. She had attractive limbs. She was graceful. She was most beautiful among the most beautiful. She was afflicted by her heavy and big hinder part. She had stout loins and breasts.

30. She was charming (to look) having beautiful red lips conquering the *bandhujīva*(flowers). She had charming row of pleasing teeth conquering a row of pearls.

31. She had a good face endowed with the lustre of manifold full moons of autumn. She had a well-parted hair. She had eyes resembling the charming autumnal lotus.

32. Her beautiful nose conquering the beak of the king of birds (Garuḍa) was captivating. She was having a pair of cheeks surpassing (the beauty of) the golden gaṇḍūka (snail).

33-34. She was having lovely ears adorned with gem-studded ornaments. She had attractive cheeks besmeared with sandal, *agallochum*, musk and saffron drops added with vermilion powder. Her well-combed locks of hair was adorned with a garland of *mālatī* (flowers).

35. She was having a heavy, fragrant and beautiful braids of hair. She had a pair of feet annoying the lustre of the land lotus.

36. She had a gait putting to shame gander and wag-tail. (She was wearing) an attractive garland of wild flowers set with excellent gems.

37. (She was wearing) a necklace set with diamonds, gem-studded bracelets on the upper arms and wrist. She had a beautiful gem-studded die.

38. She had beautiful feet decorated with varied designs and adorned with chiming anklets set with invaluable gems.

39. After conversing with (Lord) Govinda (Kṛṣṇa), she sat on an excellent throne, looking at the lotus-face of her husband with a smile.

40. Then manifested at once from her (Rādhā's) pores host of cowherdesses similar to her in their forms and attire.

41. The numbered lac-crores Goloka as counted by experts in reckoning. They had always permanent maidenhood.

42-43. O sage ! Then manifested at once a host of cowherds resembling (Lord) Kṛṣṇa in their forms and dress from his pores. They were handsome and attractive. They were reckoned as thirty crores by experts in counting.

44-45. Then there arose at once a host of cows of varied colours and perennially young from the pores of (Lord) Kṛṣṇa. (The host of cows consisted of) bulls, cows and calves of different kinds. They were auspicious. The wish yielding cows were much graceful, dark and manifold.

46. One of the bulls attractive and equal in its strength to a crore lions, Kṛṣṇa gave to Śiva for (being used as) a vehicle.

47. Then there came into being at once a row of attractive gander together with the female, male and young ones from the fissures in the toe-nails.

48. One of them, a royal one, strong and valorous, Kṛṣṇa gave to Brahmā, the ascetic, for (being used as) a vehicle.

49. Then manifested a host of attractive white horses from the left ear-hole of (Lord) Kṛṣṇa, the Supreme Being.

50. Then the Lord of the cowherdesses gave away with pleasure one of the white horses to Dharma, for (being used as) a vehicle, in the presence of the host of celestials.

51. Then came into being a row of strong and valorous male lions from the right ear-hole (of Lord Kṛṣṇa) in the midst of the host of celestials.

52. (Lord) Kṛṣṇa gave away one of them to *prakṛti*. He bestowed on her a revered garland set with invaluable gem and the desired boon.

53. Kṛṣṇa, the adept in yoga, made five chariots by meditation. They were made of pure and excellent gems. They were attractive and capable of moving at will.

54. Extending to a lac *yojanas* above and hundred *yojanas* at the top, they had a lac wheels. They were swift as the wind. They were equipped with a lac of pleasure-houses.

55. They were endowed with numerous bed-steads and materials for enjoyment fit for making love. They were illuminated by a lac of gem-studded lamps and horses.

56. They had plenty of various kinds of wonderful pictures. They were radiant with pitchers studded with quality gems. They were equipped with gem-studded mirrors and ornaments. They were adorned with white chowries.

57. They were adorned with garments as pure as fire and collection of pearls. They were radiant with necklace made of excellent gems, pearls, rubies and diamonds.

58. They were decorated with numerous beautiful artificial lotuses red in colour and having the hue of sapphire.

59. O foremost among the brahmins! One among them he gave to Nārāyaṇa. After having given one to Rādhikā, he reserved the rest for himself.

60-61. A tawny-coloured person then manifested from the organ of generation of Kṛṣṇa together with a host of tawny-coloured beings. Since they manifested from the private organ they were known as the *guhyakas.* That male person was Kubera, the Lord of wealth and the master of the *guhyakas.*

62. A maiden came into being from the left-side of Kubera. That goddess was the consort of Kubera and was (known as) Manoramā (lovely) among the beautiful women.

63. Ghosts, spirits, goblins, *kūṣmāṇḍas, brahmarākṣasas,* and *vetālas* (different kinds of goblins), the deformed beings, were born from the private organ of (Kubera).

64-65. O sage ! Then there manifested the companions (of Kṛṣṇa) from His face. They were all holding conch, disc, mace, and lotus. They were wearing garlands of wild flowers. They were clad in yellow dress. They had dark complexion and four arms. They were crowned and they had ear-pendants. They were adorned with gemmed ornaments.

66. He gave away the four-armed companions to Nārāyaṇa, the *guhyakas* to Guhyakeśa and ghosts and others to Śaṅkara.

67-69. Then there manifested *vaiṣṇavas* devoted to (Lord) Kṛṣṇa. They had two arms. They had dark complexion. They were holding rosaries. They were always meditating the lotus feet of (Lord) Kṛṣṇa with pleasure. They were always engaged in serving (the Lord) offering *arghya* with earnestness. They had horripilation on their limbs, while tears swelled in their eyes, and voice was choking. They manifested from the lotus feet (of the Lord). Hence they had single devotion to the lotus feet (of the Lord).

70-72. Then there manifested frightful beings from the right eye of (Lord) Kṛṣṇa. They were wielding tridents and spears. They had three eyes and (crescent)moon on their heads. They were nude. Their bodies resembled the flames of burning fire. Those *bhairavas* were blessed. They resembled Śiva in their splendour. *Bhairavas* are known to be eight—Ruru, Saṁhāra, Kāla, Asita, Krodha, Bhīṣaṇa, Mahābhairava and Khaṭvāṅga.

73-74. Then there manifested a frightful being from the left eye of Kṛṣṇa. He was holding a trident, spear, tiger-skin-dress and mac. He was nude and had a big body with three eyes and moon on his head. That blessed one was Īśāna, the master of the guardians of the quarters.

75. Thousands of *ḍākinīs, yoginīs* and *kṣetrapālas* manifested from the nostril.

76. Thirty three crores of celestials having divine bodies manifested from the hinderpart of that person.

CHAPTER SIX

Eulogy of Śiva on Kṛṣṇa and Merits of Worship of Śiva

Sauti said :

1-2. Then (Lord) Kṛṣṇa gave away Mahālakṣmī and Sarasvatī with respect to (Lord) Nārāyaṇa together with a garland and an excellent gem. He dedicated with respect Sāvitrī to (Lord) Brahmā, Mūrti to Dharma, the beautiful Rati to Kāma and Manoramā to Kubera.

3-4. Kṛṣṇa dedicated other beautiful women to those respectively from whom they had originated. Then the Supreme Lord beckoned Śaṅkara, the preceptor of the yogins, and spoke endearing words, 'May you accept (the goddess) riding the lion'.

5. Listening to the words of Śrī Kṛṣṇa, Nīlalohita (Śiva) smiled and replied after prostration the undecaying master and Lord of life with fright.

Śrī Maheśvara said :

6-10. 'Like ordinary people I do not accept *prakṛti* now (as my bride). She is opposed to devotion to you. She is a hindrance to the path of service. She is the gate for the doorway of meditation that shuts the knowledge of truth. She is of the form of destruction of the desire for liberation. She is overwhelmed with desire. She increases the desire. She forms a veil for asceticism. She is a box of great illusion. She is securedly imprisoned in the terrible mundane existence. She always gives rise to wrong notions. She destroys right notions. She always promotes the desire for securing trifling objects of the world. O Lord I do not desire to have her as my wife. Grant me my desired boon. A good master grants one the desired (fruit).

11. There is always growing desire in your service and devotion to you. I do not get satisfied in repetition (of name) and service at your feet.

12. I roam about singing always your name and quality that is the abode of all auspiciousness with my five faces while I am asleep and awake.

13-14. May I be bent on meditating your form for a crore of *kalpa* (period). Let me never have desire for enjoyment. May my mind be drawn towards meditation and penance, in your service, worship, salutation and repetition of (your) name. May my mind be drawn towards these always. If there is any break I will be disturbed.

15-16. O Conferer of boons ! Grant me these nine kinds of devotion— Remembrance of yourself, recital of your names, narration of your virtues, listening to your virtues, repetition of your name, contemplation of your graceful form, adoration of your feet, surrender of one's self (at your service) and daily partaking of offerings made to you'.

17. "O Lord! Those liberated souls conversant with liberation speak about six kinds of liberation—possessing the same power (as the Lord), residence in the same place, having the same form, being in the vicinity (of the Lord) and union leading to total resemblance.

18-20a. Powers of becoming as small as the atom, becoming light, attaining anything, doing as one desires, increasing one's size, supremacy, subduing passions, termination of all desires, omniscience, listening to far-off (sounds), entering another's body, perfect speech, (becoming) wish-yielding tree, creation, destruction, superiority, immortality and being foremost of all are known to be the eighteen perfections.

20b-24. Meditations, penances, charities, austerities, glory and fame, truthful words, righteous practices, fasting, making pilgrimages, bathing, adoration of new gods, adoration of gods, holy sight of the seven continents, circumambulation seven times, bathing in seven oceans, beholding all the heavens, positions of Brahmā, Rudra and Viṣṇu, Supreme position and whatever other utterances that are desired; all these which have been described do not deserve (the merits of) a sixteenth part of devotion to you."

25. After listening to the words of Śarva (Śiva), (Lord), Kṛṣṇa smiled and told that preceptor of meditators true words comforting him.

The Lord said :

26. "O master of all the beings ! Śarva! Foremost among Omniscient ones ! You render service to me day and night for a full period of crore *kalpas.*[1]

27. O Lord of the celestials ! You are outstanding among the ascetics, accomplished ones, those who meditate, learned ones, devotees of Viṣṇu and the celestials.

28-30. O Bhava (Śiva)! You attain immortality. You become the great conqueror of death." O child! You will accomplish all tasks, know the *vedas* and attain omniscience by my favour. You will behold the fall of innumerable Brahmās on account of my sport'. 'O Śiva! You become equal to me by knowledge, splendour, age, valour, fame and might from today. You are dearer to me than the life. There is no one more devoted to me than yourself.

31-32. There is no one dearer to me than yourself. You are superior to my soul. Whoever despise you, those perverse sinners devoid of knowledge, would get entangled in the snare of time so long as the Sun and Moon end of hundred crores of *kalpas.*

33-35. It is proper for you to honour my words so that they do not go in vain. You have made a statement 'I will not do now'. You will honour my statement and your statement. O Śambhu (Śiva)! after accepting *prakṛti*, you will enjoy happiness for thousand divine years. There is no doubt that you will make love. You are not only a great ascetic but you are a great master like me.

36. You are a householder or an ascetic or meditator as days pass at your self-will. You have stated that you will have grief if you take a wife.

37. Only a wicked woman gives grief, but not a chaste woman. One who is born in a good family is known as kulajā (born in a good family) and a protector of the family.

38-41. She takes care of the husband with affection just as (she would do for) a good son. For women from good families the husband is the kinsman, master and god whether one is degraded or not and whether one is poor or rich. Those born in family of bad reputation, possessing the bad traits of their fathers, the vile woman, would certainly be wanton and censure their husbands always. A chaste woman who regards her husband more than either of us would rejoice with her husband in the Goloka for a crore *kalpas*. O Śiva! That *prakṛti* would become later as Śivā devoted to Śiva or Viṣṇu.

42-47. At my bidding you will take that pious woman as your wife for your well-being. One who makes thousand (replicas) of your *liṅga* (emblem of Śiva) encircled by (the replicas) of the female organ of *prakṛti* out of earth from a sacred place and worships them well at a sacred place with devotion offering five kinds of services (such as offering flowers, incense, lamp etc.), together with gifts, such a pure, self-controlled one that has conquered his senses, would rejoice in the Goloka with me for a crore *kalpa* periods. One that worships a lac (*liṅgas*) at a sacred place as laid down and offers gifts, would never be ousted from Goloka. He would become equal to us. Whoever makes a *liṅga* of earth, ash, cow-dung, mud or sand at a sacred place and offers worship once, he would reside in the heaven for ten thousand *kalpa* periods. One would be blessed with progeny, landed property, knowledge, sons and kinsmen, and liberation by the worship of the Śiva-*liṅga*. The spot where the Śiva-*liṅga* is worshipped is a sacred spot of mine. It would be a sacred place. Whoever dies there, even if he be a sinner, he would attain the world of Śiva.

48. With great fight I go after a person repeating (the names) Mahādeva, being greedy of listening to the name.

49. Whoever discards his life uttering the word *śiva*, would free from sins accrued in crore births and would attain liberation.

50. (The word) *śiva* expresses auspiciousness. Auspicious expresses liberation. Since that (liberation) is the outcome of that (auspiciousness), He is said to be *śiva*.

51. When there is separation from wealth or kinsmen, or when one is drowned in the ocean of grief, one would obtain everything good by repeating the word '*śiva*'.

52. (The letter) '*śi*' implies destruction of sins and (the letter) '*va*' confers liberation. Hence *śiva* is proclaimed as the destroyer of sins and bestower of liberation.

53. In whose speech the auspicious name *śiva* is present, the sins accrued by him in crores of births would certainly get destroyed."

54. After having spoken thus to Śiva, Kṛṣṇa granted Him the sacred formula, that is the wish-yielding tree and true knowledge conquering death. He then spoke to (goddess) Siṁhavāhinī.

The Lord said :

55. "O child ! You stay now in Goloka in my presence. You will attend upon Śiva in course of time. The abode of Śiva confers auspiciousness.

56. O Lady having a beautiful face ! After having manifested in the splendour of all the celestials and killed all the demons, you will be worshipped by all.

57. Then in the *kalpa* called *satya*, when the *satyayuga* prevails, you will become the daughter of Dakṣa possessing good traits and the mistress of Śambhu (Śiva).

58. Then when your husband is censured in the sacrifice, you would discard your life and you would be born as Pārvatī to Menā, the wife of the Mountain (Himavān).

59. You would sport with Lord Śambhu (Śiva) for thousand divine years and then you would attain total identity (with Him) all the time.

60. O Goddess of the celestials ! You will be worshipped in all the worlds at the time of great adorations in autumn every year.

61. You will be worshipped as the village goddess or goddess of the town with different attractive designations.

62. At my bidding your worship will be performed according to different kinds of *tantras* made by Śiva. I will explain you the mode of worship and amulet together with the hymn.

63. Great people would become your attendants. The accomplishers of piety, wealth, desire and liberation would attain the fruits.

64. O mother ! Whoever worship you in the holy land of Bhārata, their fame, glory, piety and wealth would flourish."

65. After having spoken to *prakṛti* thus He imparted the excellent sacred formula of eleven syllables together with the desired seed-letter forming its essential part.

66. Out of compassion for His devotees, He formulated a mode of meditation for the devotees and again imparted a sacred formula of ten syllables endowed with mystic charm and desired seed-letter.

67. The Lord blessed her with the power useful for creation, all abilities to accomplish the desires and the foremost true knowledge.

68. O Brahmin ! The Lord of the universe then conferred on her the sacred formula of thirteen syllables and imparted a mystic amulet together with an eulogy to (Lord) Śaṅkara (Śiva).

69. After having blessed Dharma with that formulae, that is the knowledge leading to accomplishment, (he blessed) Kāma, Fire-god, Kubera and Vāyu.

70. After having imparted the excellent formulae etc., to Kubera and others then, He directed Brahmā for the purpose of creation. He is the ordainer of Brahmā.

The Lord said :

71. "O Brahmā ! The Fortunate one! You practise penance pertaining to me for thousand divine years and make the different types of creation.

72. After having spoken to Brahmā thus, Kṛṣṇa bestowed a garland on Manoramā, and proceeded to Vṛndāvana in the company of the cowherds and cowherdesses.

CHAPTER SEVEN

The Creation of the Worlds

Sauti said :

1. Then Brahmā practised penance and attained the desired perfection. He then created the earth at first from the fat of (demons) Madhu and Kaiṭabha.

2-3. He created eight charming chief mountains. The minor ones were numerous. How can I describe (them all)? Listen (to my narration)of the chief ones. (They are) Sumeru, Kailāsa, Malaya, Himālaya, Udaya, Asta, Suvela and Gandhamādana.

4-5. He created the seven oceans, numerous female and male rivers.[1] (He then created) the trees, villages and cities. Listen to the names of the oceans Lavaṇa, Ikṣu, Surā, Sarpis, Dadhi, Dugdha and Jala. The extent of the first one is a lakh *yojanas.* The subsequent ones are twice the preceding ones.

6. (He then created) the seven continents on the lotus-shaped earth. (Then he created) the seven minor continents and seven boundary mountains.

7. O Brahmin ! You (now) know from me the names of the seven continents created by Brahmā in the past. They are Jambū, Śāka, Kuśa, Plakṣa, Krauñca, Nyagrodha (Śālmali) and Puṣkara.

8. The Lord created eight beautiful cities on the eight peaks of Meru for the enjoyments of the eight guardian deities of the world.

9. The Lord of the world then created the city of Ananta at the root (of Meru) and then the seven heavens above. Listen to (the narration of) their names.

10. O Śaunaka ! (they are) Bhūrloka, Bhuvarloka, Svarloka the beautiful, Janoloka, Tapoloka and Satyaloka .

11. The Brahmaloka is on the top of the peak. It is devoid of old age etc. The Dhruvaloka is above that. It is charming all round.

12. The Lord of the world created the seven nether worlds, below that. O Sage! They are full of enjoyable things surpassing those found in the heaven. They are below the other in order.

13. (They are) Atala, Vitala, Sutala, Talātala, Mahātala, Pātāla and Rasātala.

14. The universal egg consisting of the seven continents, seven heavens and seven nether worlds is governed by Brahmā.

15. There are several such universal eggs. O Śaunaka! All are artificially made in the pores of Mahāviṣṇu.

16. The guardian deities, Brahmā, Viṣṇu, Maheśvara, celestials and men and others are due to the illusion of (Lord) Kṛṣṇa.

17. The Lord of the world (Brahmā), Śaṅkara, Dharma and Viṣṇu are incapable of counting the universal eggs. Then what (to speak) about the celestials ?

18-19. The Lord is able to count them. Though He is capable, He has no inclination to count. Although He is capable (of counting), the universe, ethereal region, the quarters and all around, the universes and those contained in the universe are artificial. O Foremost Brahmin! They are transitory and are perishable like a dream.

20. The Vaikuṇṭha, Śivaloka and Goloka above them are eternal. They are outside the universe. They are similar to the quarters of the soul's space.

CHAPTER EIGHT

The Creation of the Sages and the Mutual Curses of Brahmā and Nārada

Sauti said :

1. After having created the universe, Brahmā impregnated his loving spouse Sāvitrī just as a lustful person would do for a lustful wife.

2-3. She bore the unbearable foetus for hundred divine years. She had a good delivery and gave birth to charming four *vedas* and different collections of sciences such as the Logic, Grammar etc. The fascinating divine *rāgiṇis* (modifications of musical modes) number thirty two.

4-6. O Ascetic ! (she created) the six beautiful musical nodes together with different measures of time(in music), the *satya* (*yuga*), *tretā* (*yuga*), *dvāpara* (*yuga*) and the *kali* (*yuga*) desirous of (creating)strife. (She generated)the year, month, seasons, days, *daṇḍa* (a cubit), moment etc., day, night, week, twilight and dawn. (She created) Puṣṭi, Devasenā, Medhā, Vijaya, Jayā, the six *kṛttikās*, yogas (periods of time), Karaṇa (a division of the day).

7. The chaste Devasenā, (known as) Mahāṣaṣṭhi (also) and dear spouse of Kārtikeya, chief among the mothers is the favourite deity of children.

8-9. The three *kalpaṣ* known as Brahma, Pādma and Vārāha, the four kinds of deluges nitya(daily), *naimittika* (occasional), *parārdha* (a high number) and *prākṛta* and kāla, the daughter of Mṛtyu and all the hosts of diseases she gave birth to and suckled them.

10. Then Adharma(unrighteousness) was born from the backside of Brahmā. Alakṣmi, the extremely lustful woman, was born from the left side of Adharma.

11. Viśvakarmā, the preceptor of architects was born from his navel. (Then came into being) the eight great *vasus*, who were mighty and valorous.

12-13. The four boys aged five, shining with lustre, manifested from the mind of Brahmā. They were—Sanaka, Sananda, Sanātana the third one and the venerable Sanatkumāra, the foremost among the wise.

14-15. Then manifested from his face a handsome youth of golden complexion possessing a divine form and endowed with prosperity together with his spouse. He was the originator of the *kṣatriyas* by name Svāyambhuva Manu. That woman was Śatarūpā endowed with charming form and a part (of the beauty) of the lotus.

16-17. O Fortunate Brahmin ! Manu in the company of his wife abided the command of Brahmā. Brahmā directed his delighted sons, the great Bhāgavatas, to make creation. They refused and went away to do penance bent on (Lord) Kṛṣṇa.

18-20. Brahmā, the master of the world, became angry on account of that. From the glowing lustre of the enraged Lord Brahmā's forehead manifested eleven Rudras. Kālāgnirudra, the destroyer, is said to be one among them. He is known to be *Tāmasa* (engulfed in darkness or ignorance) among all things in the universe. Brahmā Himself is *Rājasa* (endowed with passion). (Lords) Śiva and Viṣṇu are *Sāttvika* (endowed with goodness).

21-23. Kṛṣṇa the Lord of Goloka is without any quality and is above the nature. But only the ignorant and stupid refer to Śiva as *Tāmasa* (engulfed in darkness). He is of the form of pure goodness, unstained and a foremost Vaiṣṇava (devotee of Viṣṇu). Listen to the names of Rudra referred to in the *vedas*. They are *mahān* (the great), *mahātmā* (great soul) *matimān* (possessing intellect), *Bhiṣaṇa* (frightening) *bhayaṅkara* (frightful), *ṛtudhvaja* (having the seasons as the banner), *ūrdhvakeśa* (having the hair erect), *piṅgalākṣa* (having tawny eyes), *ruci* (taste) and *śuci* (pure).

24-28. Pulastya (was born) from the right ear and Pulaha from the left ear. Atri (was born) from the right eye and Kratu from the left eye. Araṇi and Aṅgiras (were born) from the nostril and Ruci from the mouth. Bhṛgu (was born) from the left side and Dakṣa from the right side. Kardama was born from the shadow and Pañcaśikha from the navel. Voḍhu (was born) from the breast and Nārada from the neck. Marīci (was born) from the shoulder region and Apāntara-tamas from the throat. Vasiṣṭha (was born) from the region of tongue and Pracetas from the lower lip. Haṁsa (was born) from the left belly and Yati from the right belly. Brahmā ordered his sons to carry on creation. After listening to the words of his father, Nārada replied him.

Nārada said :

29-30. O Great Śiva ! Call my elders Sanaka and others first. O Lord of the world! After solemnising their marriage speak to us. While they have been enjoined by the father for doing penance, how (is it proper) for you to involve ourselves in worldly affairs? Alas ! The intellect of the Lord becomes perverted.

31. (It is a surprise) that you have now conferred upon some of your sons asceticism superior to nectar and bestow now on others mundane existence more dreadful than poison.

32. O Sire ! (You know pretty well) that there is no escape even after a crore *kalpa* period elapses for a person fallen into the deep and dreadful ocean of mundane existence.

33-35. Which ignorant person will divert his mind towards destructive matter rejecting the sole saviour of all, the root-cause of all, the foremost person, the bestower of all things, the conferer of devotion, the giver of servitude, the truth, the embodiment of compassion, the sole refuge of the devotees, one that is kind to worshippers, pure, one that loves the devotees, the Lord of the worshippers, the person that blesses the worshippers, one that is to be propitiated and one that can be attained ?

36-38. Which fool would reject service to (Lord) Kṛṣṇa that is more beloved than nectar and consume the adverse poison known as matter ? It is perishable like dream, insignificant, unreal and the cause of death. O Sire! Just like the tip of flame of fire attractive for the insects, a piece of flesh attached to the hook allures the fish, similarly matter is the cause of death of sensual men.

39. After having spoken thus, Nārada, resembling the tip of the flame of glowing fire, stopped and stood in front of Brahmā after prostration.

40. O Brahmin ! Becoming enraged Brahmā cursed his son. With trembling body, red face and quivering lips he spoke.

Brahmā said :

41-48. O Nārada ! You will be deprived of your knowledge on account of my curse. Like a sportive fawn, you will be dissolute loved by lustful women. You will be the dear husband of fifty loving women, endowed with good form, bloom of maidenhood and charm. You will be well-versed in the art of eroticism and greatly fond of love making. You will be the preceptor of preceptors of experts in the different methods of love-making. You will be foremost among the *Gandharvas.* You will be possessing a good voice and be a good singer. You will be a youth proficient in the appropriate time for playing on the lute. There is no doubt that you will be wise, sweet-speaking, tranquil, possessing good conduct, beautiful and an intellectual person. You will be known by the name Upabarhaṇa. After having sported with them for a lakh divine *yugas* in a desolate forest, you will be born as the son of a slave on account of my curse. O Child ! After that life, you will again be born as my son, on account of the contact wth devotees of Viṣṇu, partaking of remnant of food taken by devotees of Viṣṇu and the favours of (Lord) Kṛṣṇa. I will again be conferring on you the original divine knowledge as before. You will now cease to be my son and fall (into the mundane existence).

49. O Brahmin ! Brahmā, the master of the world, after having spoken thus to his son kept quiet. Nārada wept and with folded palms addressed his father.

Nārada said :

50. "O Father ! The preceptor of the world! Restrain your anger. Alas! This wrath towards me is not nice of you, the protector, destroyer, ascetic and master (of the world).

51. A learned person would curse and abandon his son doing wrong deed. O learned one! How is it proper on your part to curse your ascetic son ?

52. O Brahmā ! May I be born in any famly. May you grant me the boon that devotion to Hari (Lord Nārayaṇa) may never discard me.

53. Bring born as the son of Brahmā if one does not have devotion to the feet of (Lord) Hari, that wretch is inferior to a hog in this holy land of Bhārata.

54. Anyone, though born as a hog, if he remembers his former life and is endowed with devotion to Lord Hari, that foremost one would enter the Goloka by virtue of his good deeds.

55. The earth becomes consecrated by the touch of the devotees of Viṣṇu who drink the honey of devotion from the lotus feet of (Lord) Govinda.

56. O Venerable Sire ! The sacred places desire to have the touch of the devotees of Viṣṇu for washing away the sins of the sinners and themselves.

57. Soon after initiation in the mystic formula the name of Hari, people get liberated along with crores of ancestors in Bhārata.

58. Soon after initiation people get rid of the sins accrued in the course of crore of previous births, become pure and destroy (the fruits of) the actions of previous (births).

59. Whoever show the good paths to sons, wives, disciples, attendants and relatives, those would certainly attain felicity.

60. The preceptor that has earned the confidence of his pupils and shows them unrighteous path would stay in the *kumbhīpāka* (hell) till the Sun and Moon (shine).

61. A person unable to have devotion to the lotus feet of (Lord) Śrī Kṛṣṇa is a bad preceptor, vile father, wicked master and wretched son.

62. O Four-faced one ! I have been cursed by you for no offence of mine. It is proper for me to curse you. Learned injure those who injure.

63. Your mystic worship consisted of amulets, hymns and established methods. Your worship in all the worlds would certainly cease on account of my curse.

64. O Father ! May you not be worshipped in the universe for three *kalpa* (periods). After the lapse of three *kalpa* (periods) you will be worshipped well.

65. O Disciplined one! You (will be entitled) to your share now in the sacrificial offerings and austerities. But (other privileges) such as worship will cease. But you will be adored by the celestials."

66. After having spoken thus Nārada kept quiet in front of his father. Brahmā remained overwhelmed with grief in the assembly of gods.

67-68. O Śaunaka! Nārada being cursed by his father thus became a *Gandharva* by name Upabarhaṇa and the son of a slave later. Then Nārada became a great sage again and gained knowledge from his father. I will narrate you that now.

CHAPTER NINE

The Further Creation of Other Beings

Sauti said :

1. Then Brahmā asked his sons to create. O Foremost Brahmin ! Except Nārada all the others carried on the creation.

2. The patriarch Kaśyapa was born from the mind of Marīci. Moon was born in the milky ocean from the mucus of the eyes.

3. Gautama was born from the mind of Pracetas. Maitrāvaruṇa was the son of Pulastya.

4. Three daughters Ākūti, Devahūti and Prasūti were born from Manu through Śatarūpa. They (were) all chaste.

5. Two handsome sons Priyavata and Uttānapāda (were also born of him). Dhruva, the son of Uttānapāda, was very pious.

6. Ākūti was given in marriage to Ruci, Prasūti to Dakṣa and Devahūti to Kardama. Kapila was his son.

7-8. Sixty daughters were born to Dakṣa and Prasūti. He gave away eight to Dharma, eleven to Rudra, Satī to Śiva, thirteen to Kaśyapa and twenty seven to the Moon.

9. O Brahmin ! Listen to my narration of the names of the wives of Dharma. They were Śānti, Puṣṭi, Dhṛti, Tuṣṭi, Kṣamā, Śraddhā, Mati and Smṛti.

10-11. Santoṣa was the son of Śānti. Mahān was the son of Puṣṭi. Dhairya was known to be the son of Dhṛti and Harṣa and Darpa as the sons of Tuṣṭi. Sahiṣṇu (was) the son of Kṣamā. Dhārmika (was) the son of Śraddhā. Mati had a son named Jñāna. Jātismara, the great, (was the son) of Smṛti.

12. The sages Nara and Nārāyaṇa (were born) from his first wife Mūrti. O Śaunaka ! These sons of Dharma were pious.

13-14. Now you attentively listen to the names of the wives of Rudra. (They are) Kalā, Kalāvati, Kāṣṭhā, Kālikā, Kalahapriyā, Kandalī, Bhūṣaṇa, Rāsnā, Pramocā, Bhūṣaṇā and Śuki. Many sons born to them were the retinue of Śiva.

15. That Satī discarded her life at the sacrifice (hearing) the despise of her husband. She was again born as the daughter of the mountain (Himavān) and obtained Śaṅkara as her husband.

16-18. O Pious one ! Listen to the names of the spouses of Kaśyapa— Aditi, the mother of the gods, Diti, the mother of the demons; Kadrū, the mother of serpents; Vinatā; the mother of the birds; Surabhi; the mother of cows and buffaloes, and

Saramā, the mother of quadrupeds such as the dogs etc. Danu gave birth to *dānavas*. Other (wives gave birth) to other beings.

19. O Sage ! Indra, the twelve *ādityas*, Upendra and others are known to be the sons of Aditi. They were very strong and valorous.

20-21. O Brahmin ! Jayanta was the son of Indra born through Śacī. Two sons Śanaiścara and Yama and a daughter Kālindī were born to Āditya through Savarṇā, daughter of Viṣvakarmā. Maṅgala was born to Upendra and Pṛthvī (Earth).

Śaunaka said :

22. O Sauti ! It befits you to describe me how the powerful Maṅgala was born to Upendra and Vasundharā (Pṛthvī).

Sauti said :

23-25. Beholding the beautiful form of Upendra, Vasundharā got smitten by love. She assumed the form of a beautiful maiden in her full bloom, clad in charming attire and with a smile approached suddenly the handsome, good-natured and tranquil Upendra, besmeared with sandal paste and adorned with gem-studded ornaments reclining on a bed with a gentle smile in the desolate Malaya forest abound with the attractive foliage of sandal trees.

26. That lady with charming face gave him a beautiful garland of Mālatī (flowers) together with fragrant sandal paste and attractive musk and saffron.

27. Knowing her mind that the beautiful woman is smitten by love, Upendra made different kinds of amorous sports with her.

28. Then that chaste woman became unconscious on account of physical union with him. As Hari impregnated her, she (remained) as if dead or asleep.

29-30. Then that foremost person (Upendra) embraced that woman with dishevelled dress, beautiful loins, unconscious on account of excess enjoyment, stout rump and large breasts with smiling (face) and kissed her. Then he left her there alone and went away.

31. O Sage ! Urvaśī passing that way enquired her about her story. Then the Earth narrated her the story (about her).

32. She was weak and unable to sustain the semen. Being afraid she threw the semen into a mine of corals.

33. Hence a boy having the colour of corals was born. That great son of Nārāyaṇa was resembling the Sun in his lustre.

34. Medhā was the wife of Maṅgala. His son Ghaṇṭeśvara was valiant, possessing splendour and on par with (Lord) Viṣṇu.

35. Extremely powerful Hiraṇyakaśipu and Hiraṇyākṣa (were the sons) of Diti. O Brahmin! Simhikā was her daughter. Saiṁhkeya was her son.

36. Simhikā was (known as) Nirrti also. Hence Rāhu was (known as) Nairṛta. Hiraṇyākṣa (was killed) by the Boar (Viṣṇu's form). He died as a youth without progeny.

37. Prahlāda, the son of Hiraṇyakaśipu, was a foremost devotee of Viṣṇu. Virocana was his son and his son was Bali.

38. (Bāṇa), the son of Bali was a great ascetic, learned and a devotee of (Lord) Śiva. I have described you the lineage of Diti. Listen to my (narration) of the lineage of Kadrū.

39-41. O Śaunaka ! (She gave birth to) Ananta, Vāsuki, Kāliya, Dhanañjaya, Karkoṭaka, Takṣaka, Padma, Airāvata, Mahāpadma, Śaṅku, Saṁvaraṇa, Dhṛtarāṣṭra, Durdharṣa, Durjaya, Durmukha, Bala, Gokṣa, Gokārmuka and other innumerable species of snakes.

42. Goddess Manasā, born from a part of the lotus, was foremost among ascetics endowed with lustre and auspiciousness.

43. Jaratkāru, born in the family of Nārāyaṇa was her husband. Āstīka was her son equal in splendour to (Lord) Viṣṇu.

44. Men will not have any fear due to serpents by the mere remembrance of these names. I have described you the lineage of Kadrū. Listen to my (narration) of that of Vinatā.

45. Vainateya and Aruṇa, equal in valour to (Lord) Viṣṇu are her sons. They became (the progenitors) of all the species of birds in due course.

46. Cows and buffaloes were the progeny of Surabhi. All the dogs were the progeny of Saramā.

47. *Dānavas* and other species of beings in general were the progeny of Danu. I have described you the lineage of Kaśyapa. Listen to my (narration) of the legend of Moon.

48. Listen attentively to the names of the wives of Moon. It is an age-old and extremely rare legend in the *purāṇas.*

49-52. Aśvinī, Bharaṇī, Kṛttikā, Rohiṇī, Mṛgaśirṣā, Ārdrā, the adorable and pious Punarvasu, Puṣyā, Āśleśā, Maghā, Pūrvaphalgunī, Uttaraphalgunī, Hasta, Citrā, Svātī, Viśākhā, Anurādhikā, Jyeṣṭhā, Mūlā, Pūrvāṣāḍhā, Uttarā (ṣāḍhā), Śravaṇā, Dhaniṣṭhā, the auspicious Śatabhiṣak, Pūrvabhādrā, Uttarabhadrā and concluding with Revatī were the wives of Moon. Fortunate Rohinī among them was discriminating and outstanding.

53. She won over Moon by her coquetry. Moon in the company of Rohinī did not visit his other wives.

54. All the zealous sisters reported their father this fatal calamity and anguish inflicted upon them by their co-wife.

55. The enraged Dakṣa cursed Moon with mystic incantations. He (Moon) was at once seized by consumption by the curse of his father-in-law.

56. Getting emaciated everyday he became grief-stricken. After half of his body got reduced he sought the refuge of (Lord) Śaṅkara (Śiva).

57. Beholding the afflicted Moon seeking refuge, Śaṅkara, the ocean of compassion, kindly offered him protection.

58. He relieved him of his emaciation and offered him a place on his check. Becoming immortal and getting rid of his fear he stayed on the head of (Lord) Śiva.

59. Śiva became Candraśekhara (one bearing the Moon on the head) on account of bearing him on (his) head. There is no other refuge except Śiva in all the worlds.

60. Beholding her husband getting freed (of the effects of the curse), the daughters of Dakṣa wept again. They came to their father Dakṣa, the foremost among those having splendour, and sought his refuge.

61. Beating their limbs again and again they wept aloud. Those afflicted women told the timid son of Brahmā. The daughters of Dakṣa spoke —

62. We represented to you for gaining the prosperity with our husband. O Father ! May we have prosperity. Our husband endowed with good quality has been lost.

63. O Father ! Although we have the eyes, we find that everything is dark. Now we have known that the husband is the eye of women.

64. The husband is the only refuge for women. The husband is the life forces and prosperity. He is the cause of piety, wealth, pleasures and heaven (the four-fold goals). He is the bridge in the ocean of mundane existence.

65. The husband is (Lord) Nārāyaṇa, the austerity and age-old duty. All other deeds are in vain for them. They go against their husbands.

66-67. Bathing in all sacred waters, offering fees in sacrifices, charities, meritorious austerities, disciplined acts, worship of God, fasting and all penances do not have the sixteenth part of the merits of serving the feet of their Lords.

68. Among all her relatives, the son is dear to all women. He is only a part of the husband. The husband is superior to hundred sons.

69. A woman born in a bad family, vile and always drawn towards her paramour would hate her husband.

70. A chaste woman should revere (the husband) fallen, sick, vile, poor, vicious one, youth or old. She should not abandon him.

71-74. One who hates or rejects the virtuous or vicious husband would be subjected to torments in a (hell called) *kālasūtra* till the Sun and Moon shine. She would be bitten day and night by insects equal to dogs. She would consume the fat and flesh of the dead, drink urine when thirsty. She would be born as a vulture for crores of thousands (of births), a boar for hundred births and a quadruped for hundred births. She would then become a killer of her kinsman. Then if per chance she attains the birth as a human being by (the virtue of) her past deeds, she would certainly become a widow, indigent and sick.

75. O Son of Brahmā! Bestow on us the gift of (gaining our) husband fulfilling our desires. Like Brahmā you are capable of creating the world.

76. Listening to the words of his daughters Dakṣa approached (Lord) Śambhu (Śiva). Beholding him (Lord) Śambhu rose up (from his seat) and saluted him.

77. After blessing Him, Dakṣa spoke to that ocean of mercy. Beholding (Lord) Śiva saluting him, the invincible one gave up his wrath.

Dakṣa said :

78. "O (Lord) Śambhu! Grant me my dear son-in-law, the dear husband of my daughters more valuably than their lives."

79. "O Son-in-law! If you do not return me the Moon, my son-in-law, I will give you a dreadful curse".

80. O Brahmin! The mine of compassion and the bond of refuge heard the words of Dakṣa and replied him words sweeter than nectar.

Śiva said :

81. "Though you may reduce me to ashes or curse me, I will not surrender Moon that has sought my refuge."

82. After listening to the words of (Lord) Śiva, Dakṣa was about to curse (Lord) Śiva. (Lord) Śiva remembered (Lord) Govinda, the soul saviour in danger.

83. In the meanwhile (Lord) Kṛṣṇa assumed the form of an aged brahmin and arrived at that spot in their midst. Those two duly bowed to Him.

84. That splendid, age-old brahmin conferred good wishes on both. O Brahmin! He first spoke to Śaṅkara engulfed in total darkness.

The Lord said :

85. "O Śarva ! Among all kinsmen, there is no one dearer than one's self. O Lord of the celestials ! Protect yourself. You return Moon to Dakṣa.

86. You are outstanding among the ascetics and tranquil. You are the foremost devotee of Viṣṇu. You treat all the beings alike. You are devoid of (causing) injury and wrath.

87. Dakṣa, the son of Brahmā is irascible, haughty and strong. Only the virtuous are afraid of the haughty ones, but the haughty ones (are) never (afraid of the virtuous)."

88. After listening to the words of Nārāyaṇa, Śaṅkara smiled and spoke words of supreme wise counsel.

Śaṅkara said :

89. "I will give away my penance, lustre, all perfections, prosperity and life. But I am not capable of giving away a refuge.

90. If a person surrenders a refugee out of fear, virtue discards him after dreadfully cursing him.

91. O master of the world ! I am capable of abandoning all but not my own duty. A person that abandons his own duty is forsaken by all.

92. Whoever always protects righteousness, that righteousness will protect him. O Īśvara! You know the righteous way of life. Then why do you deceitfully speak to me thus.

93. You are the mother of all the beings. You are the creator and destroyer after lapse of time. A person having firm faith in you will have fear from no one."

94. The Lord Hari the knower of the dispositions of all, listened to the words of Śaṅkara and pulled out half the Moon[1] from Moon and gave him away to Dakṣa.

95. Half of Moon free from any disease on the head of Śiva departed. The progenitor seized half the Moon given by Viṣṇu.

96. Dakṣa eulogised Mādhava beholding that part (of Moon) afflicted by consumption. Hari made him full in a fortnight and emaciated in a fortnight.

97. O Brahmin ! After conferring a boon on them, Kṛṣṇa went away to his abode. Accepting the Moon, Dakṣa gave him again to his daughters.

98. The Moon got all of them and sported with them day and night. Being afraid (of Dakṣa) he bestowed equal attention to all of them then onwards.

99. O Sage ! I have described you thus a little of the process of creation that I have heard from the mouth of the preceptor at Puṣkara in the assembly of sages.

CHAPTER TEN

The Origin of the Different Castes

Sauti said :

1. Cyavana and Śukra, the foremost among the learned, were the sons of Bhṛgu. Kriyā, the wife of Kratu, gave birth to the Vālakhilyas.

2. O Śaunaka ! Bṛhaspati, Utathya and Śambara, the foremost sages, were the three sons of Aṅgiras.

3. Śakti was the son of Vasiṣṭha. Parāśara was the son of Śakti. The revered Kṛṣṇa *dvaipāyana,* a form of Hari, was the son of Parāśara.

4. Śuka, the foremost among the learned and the son of Vyāsa, was a part of Śiva. Viśaśravā was the son of Pulastya whose son was Dhaneśvara.

Śaunaka said :

5. "The words of the experts in the *purāṇas* are quite incomprehensible. I could not com- prehend the statements relating to the origin of Dhaneśa (Kubera).

6. You have just now described the origin of Kubera from the Lord (Kṛṣṇa). How is it that you are now describing me a different account ?"

Sauti said :

7. "All these regents of the quarters had no doubt their origin from the Supreme Lord. Again because of the curse of Brahmā, he (was born as) the son of Viśaśravā.

8. Utathya requested a crore gold coins from Kubera in order to pay the fee to his preceptor Pracetas.

9. Kubera reluctantly gave him that (amount). The irate brahmin reduced him to ashes. He hence attained rebirth.

10. Hence Kubera, the son of Viśaśravā, is the Lord of wealth. Rāvaṇa, Kumbhakarṇa and pious Vibhīṣaṇa (were also the sons of Viśaśravā) command of Brahmā, he was born on earth to a *Brāhmaṇa* woman.

11. Vātsya was the son of Pulaha. Śāṇḍilya was the son of Ruci. Sāvarṇi was born from Gautama. He was foremost among the sages.

12. Kāśyapa was born from Kaśyapa and Bharadvāja from Bṛhaspati. Vātsya (was born) from Pulaha and Śāvarṇi from Gautama.

13. (Śāṇḍilya was the son of Ruci). He was foremost among the ascetics). (These five sages) were the founders of the five *gotras* (clans) of *brāhmaṇas.*

14. The other *brāhmaṇa* groups were born from the face of Brahmā. O Śaunaka ! Being without *gotras* (clans) they migrated to different places.

15-16. *Kṣatriyas* (Warrior castes) were known to be the descendants of Moon, Sun and Manu. The other *kṣatriyas* (were born) from the arm of Brahmā. The *vaiśyas* (were born) from the loins and the *sūdras* from the foot. The mixed castes were born from a mxture of these (castes).

17-18. O Foremost Brahmin ! The cowherds, barbers, *bhillas, modakas*[1], *kūbaras* (masons), sellers of betel, goldsmiths and merchant communities were known as *sacchūdras.* The Karaṇa was from the *vaiśya* (father) and *śūdra* (mother) and *ambaṣṭha* from the *brahmaṇa* (father) and *vaiśya* (mother).

19-21. Viśvakarmā impregnated the *śudra* women. Then the nine artisan classes *mālākāra* (florist), *śaṅkhakāra* (shell-cutter), *karmakāra* (blacksmith), *kuvindaka* (weaver), *kumbhakāra* (potter), *kāṅisyakāra* (bell-metal worker) the six foremost artisans and *sūtrakāra* (the carpenter), *citrakāra* (painter) and *svarṇakāra* (goldsmith) were born. These (three) were degraded on account of the curse of a Brahmin and these mixed castes were not fit for offering sacrificial rites.

Śaunaka said :

22-23. How did the Lord Viśvakarmā impregnate the degraded *śūdra* women ? How were the three (castes) degraded ? Why were they cursed by a brahmin ? O Foremost among those well-versed in the *purāṇas* ! You are fit to tell me.

Sauti said :

24. (Once the nymph) Ghṛtācī, being overcome by passion put on a lovely dress. Viśvakarmā beheld her on the way as she was proceeding towards Puṣkara.

25. He came there to look at her with mind blooming with delight. With passion swelling in his heart he beseeched her for sexual union.

26-31. (Viśvakarmā) well-versed in erotics spoke words pleasing the ears and capable of kindling the fire of passion to that tranquil and lovely woman on beholding her (form) adorned with gem-studded ornaments, possessing graceful limbs, having eternal maidenhood of sixteen years, suffering the heaviness of big rump, attracting the minds of sages, eyeballs rolling on account of the quickly moving side glances, tormented by passion, having hard loins, with the dress displaced by the wind, with lofty, hard, circular and elevated pair of breasts, with beautiful and smiling face surpassing the autumnal moon, with attractive lower lip deep red resembling the ripe bimba fruit, with vermilion and musk dot (on the forehead), and with sparkling cheeks adorned by pendant studded with invaluable gems.

Viśvakarmā said :

32. "O Graceful Lady! Dear to me than my life! Where do you hasten taking away my life? O Auspicious one! Stay for a while dear lady.

33. I have been wandering the world in search of you. I do not desire to discard my life in the fire without looking at you.

34. Having heard from Rambhā that you are proceeding to the world of Kāma, I have come today and stationed on your way.

35-36. My dear ! You sport with me at this lovely flower garden on the banks of Sarasvatī rendered fragrant by gentle, cool, fragrant winds. It is desirable to have the union of male and female youth.

37. Possessing eternal maidenhood you alone live forever. You are passionate, possessing graceful limbs and most beautiful.

38. On account of the favour extended by Mṛtyuñjaya (Śiva), I have won over the daughter of Yama. I repaired to the mansions of Kubera and obtained wealth from Kubera.

39. I have obtained gem-studded necklace from Varuṇa and gem-studded ornament for women from Wind god and pair of apparel as pure as fire from the radiant Fire-god.

40. (I have learnt) the Science of Erotics that delights women from God of love. A little of the art of love-making, that is rare, I have gained from the Moon.

41. The moment I had obtained the gem-studded necklace, the pair of apparel and all the ornaments, I had mentally decided to give them to you.

42. Dear One ! I have placed them in the mansion and come in search of you. I will give them to you now when we retire enjoying sexual union."

43. O Sage ! Ghṛtācī quickly replied smilingly sweet words of good counsel after listening to the words of the passionate one.

Ghṛtācī said:

44. "What you had spoken, I accept it as good and excellent. But O Love-sick one ! I will describe you an engagement that I have to keep up.

45. I am proceeding to the abode of God of love and I have dressed myself for that purpose. (Our practice is) that the day anyone of us goes to anyone, on that particular day she is regarded as his wife.

46. Today, I am the spouse of God of love. Hence I am the wife of your preceptor. What you have spoken to me now, you have learnt it from the God of love.

47. The preceptor imparting knowledge and the preceptor initiating in mystic syllables is a lac of times greater than the father and thousand times greater than the mother. There is no other preceptor equal in merits to him.

48. It has been mentioned in the *vedas* that the wife of the preceptor is to be revered hundred times more than the preceptor. O Wise one ! The mother is to be revered hundred times more than the father.

49. It has been declared in the *vedas* that the ravishment of the preceptor's wife is hundred times more scandalous than the violation of the mother by the son.

50. A lady addressed as the mother by a person is equivalent to the mother. God of virtue can testify this.

51. A person ravishing such a lady goes (to the hell called) *kālasūtra.* He remains in that dreadful (hell) till the Sun and Moon (shine).

52. Ravishing one's mother is four times more sinful than that. Ravishing one's preceptor's wife is a lac times (more scandalous).

53. Such a person falls into the *kumbhīpāka* (hell) for a period of Brahmā's life. It has never been heard in the *veda* about any atonement for such sinners.

54-55. *kumbhīpāka* has been described as the place of sinners. It has the shape of a potter's wheel with sharp edges like the sword. It abounds with fat, urine and faeces. It has insects like the trident and hot lave equal to fire.

56. Whatever sin accrues to a person ravishing his preceptor's wife, similar (sin accrues to) the preceptor's wife if she has carnal desires.

57. I am now going to the abode of God of love as his wife. On some other day I will dress myself and come to you."

58. After listening to the words of Ghṛtācī, Viśvakarmā got enraged and cursed her 'You take birth as a *śūdra* on the earth'.

59. After listening to those words, Ghṛtācī gave him a dreadful curse: 'Fall from heaven and be born on the earth'.

60. After speaking thus to Viśvakarmā, Ghṛtācī repaired to the abode of God of love. After enjoying the union with Kāma she narrated him what had happened.

61. O Śaunaka ! On the words of Kāma, she was born from the wife of the cowherd Madana in the city of Prayāga.

62. As she had remembrance of the lineage of her past life, she was an ascetic. That pious lady did not seek any boon and had her mind bent on doing penance.

63. Resembling the colour of heated gold on account of penance, she did penance for hundred years on the captivating banks of the Ganges.

64. Subsequently she gave birth to nine sons from the energy of Viśvakarmā and once again became Ghṛtācī after her return to Svaloka.

Śaunaka said :

65. How did that ascetic woman bear the energy of Viśvakarmā and where and how long after she give birth to nine sons ?

Sauti said :

66. After listening to her curse, Viśvakarmā became angry, hastened to Brahma's place heart filled with remorse.

67. After prostrating and eulogizing Brahmā, he narrated him what had happened. By the command of Brahmā, he was born on earth to a *brāhmaṇa* woman.

68. He became a brahmin and an expert artisan on the earth. He constructed different mansions for the kings and householders.

69. He constructed all types of houses for all, all the time all around. (He built) wonderful and beautiful houses of different kinds.

70-71 Once upon a time after doing the crafts for a king at Prayāga, he proceeded to the Ganges and beheld the lovely woman Ghṛtācī as an ascetic maiden in her new form. O Brahmin ! Remembering his original lineage, he recognized her conscious of her past lineage.

72. On beholding her his heart being drawn towards her, his passion was kindled. That tranquil person spoke sweet words to that calm ascetic woman.

The Brahmin said :

73-74. "Ah Wonder ! O Ghṛtācī ! Beautiful one! You are here only. O Attractive one ! Do you not remember me? I am Viśvakarmā. I will redeem you from the curse. O Charming one ! You entertain me as yours. The god of love is tormenting me. My mind is pining for you.

75. Listening to the words of the brahmin, the calm Ghṛtācī in her new form, spoke to him sweet and excellent words of good counsel.

The Cowherdess said :

76. That day I was the spouse of Kāma (God of love). Now I am an ascetic. How can I have union with you on (the holy) banks of Ganges in Bhārata ?

77. O Viśvakarmā ! Bhārata is meritorious and a place of deeds. Whatever deed is done here it would be giving enjoyment elsewhere whether it be good or bad.

78. Pious people take birth here as a result of their asceticism for the sake of redemption. But being deluded by the illusion of (Lord) Viṣṇu, one gets bound and does deeds.

79. Whoever satisfies the illusion of Viṣṇu and Īśāna, (Lord) Śrīkṛṣṇa confers on him devotion and the favourite mystic syllable.

80. A person being born in Bhārata, getting drawn towards worldly pleasures, forgetting the Supreme Lord Kṛṣṇa and getting stupefied on account of the illusion of Viṣṇu, is a fool.

81. O Lord ! I remember everything. Good luck ! I remember my previous birth. I was formerly Ghṛtācī, the celestial nymph. Now I am a cowherdess.

82. I am doing penance on this meritorious banks of the Ganges for the sake of liberation. This is not the place for dalliance. O Passionate one ! You be at rest.

83. A sin done elsewhere gets destroyed on the Ganges. But a sin committed on the banks of the Ganges gets at once multiplied a lac-fold.

84. A sin that has been committed out of passion gets destroyed by penance only at a sacred place of Nārāyaṇa, and one becomes the old self again.

85. After listening to the words of Ghṛtācī, Viśvakarmā like the wind in his stature, held her and carried her off to the Malaya (forest), abode of the sandal (trees).

86-87. He enjoyed her company for twelve years, unaware of the day and night, in a lonely forest in the Malaya valley, on a charming flower-bed made fragrant by the wind (carrying the fragrance) of flowers and sandal.

88. The pregnancy of that lovely woman attained its fullness and (became) unbearable. She delivered nine handsome sons at that place itself.

89-90. O Śaunaka! They were the florists, blacksmiths, shell-cutters, weavers, potters, carpenters, goldsmiths and painters,[1] well-instructed architects, endowed with knowledge, strong and wise on account of their past good deeds.

91. Those two returned to their respective original places after conferring boons on them and establishing them on the earth discarding their mortal coil.

92. O Foremost Brahmin ! The Goldsmith had at once fallen on account of stealing the gold of brahmins by the curse of a brahmin.

93. The carpenter was degraded on the earth for not having made ready the fuel for the sacrifice by the curse of the brahmins.

94. On account of transgressing (the contracts) in respect of the paintings, the painter was at once degraded by the curse of a brahmin on account of the wrath of the brahmins.

95. On account of association with the goldsmith, a particular merchant-class was degraded for the offence of stealing gold and the like on account of the curse of a brahmin.

96. The *aṭhālikākara* (mason) had the origin from the florist and an unchaste śudrra woman. On account of the blemish of the paramour he became degraded.

97. The koṭaka had the origin from a mason and a potter-woman. That builder of houses was at once degreaded.

98. The *tailakāra* (oilman) originated from the potter and *koṭaka* woman. He was crooked and degraded on the earth.

99. The Tīvara was born from the *kṣatriya* male and a princely woman. On account of the blemish of the paramour he was degraded.

100, The *dasyu* or *leṭa* is known to be a degraded one, born from a *tīvara* male and *tailakāra* woman.

101. *Leṭa* begot the six son *mālla, mantra, mātara, bhaṇḍa, kola* and *kalandara* through a *tīvara* maiden.

102. *Śūdra* begot on a *brāhmaṇa* maiden, a *caṇḍāla*, degraded on account of the blemish of the paramour, meanest of all and impure.

103. *carmakāra* (cobbler) was born from a *tīvara* and Caṇḍāla woman. *Māṁsaccheda* (meat-cutter) was born from a *caṇḍala* and *carmakāra* woman.

104. *Moñca* is stated to be from *tīvara* and a *māṁsaccheda* woman. *Kartāra* is said to be from *kaivata* and a *koñca* woman.

105. O Śaunaka ! The two vile castes *haḍḍi* and *ḍama* were from a Leṭa male and a *caṇḍala* maiden.

106. Five vile foresters were duly born from a *caṇḍāla* male and a *haḍḍi* maiden.

107. O Śaunaka ! A child born on the banks of the Ganges to a *leṭa* male and *tīvara* maiden was known as *gaṅgāputra.* account of their association with *haḍḍi* (community).

108. The *veṣadhārī* male begot on a *gaṅgāputra* maiden a son known as *yuṅgī.*

109. From the *vaiśya* male and *tīvara* maiden was born *śuṇḍī. Pauṇḍraka* came into being from a *vaiśya* male and *śuṇḍī* maiden.

110. From a *kṣatra* (*kṣatriya*) male and *karaṇa* maiden *rājaputra* was born. *Āgarī* is known to be from a *karaṇa* male and *rājaputrī* maiden.

111. *Kaivarta* is known to be from a *kṣatra* male and *vaiśya* woman. The *kaivartas* on account of their association with the *tīvara* in the *kali* (yuga), a degraded (caste) *dhīvara* came into being on the earth.

112. *Rajaka* is known to be from a *dhīvara* male and Tīvara maiden. *Koyāli* was born from a *tīvara* male and *rajaka* woman.

113. From a *nāpita* (barber) and a *gopa* maiden (was born) *sarvasvī. Vyādha* (hunter) was born from a *kṣatra* male and a woman of that caste (*sarvasvī*). (He is) strong and a killer of beasts.

114. Seven offspring came into being from a *tīvara* male and *śuṇḍī* woman. They on were always known in the *kali* (yuga) as *dasyus.*

115-116. A sage begot on a *brāhmaṇa* woman (by the union) on the first day of the menses a caste known as *kūḍara* because of its origin from the contemptible womb. That impure one though equal to a brahmin, was degraded on account of the blemish of the menses. On account of the association with the *koṭaka* it was considered the lowest in the world.

117-118. A *kṣatriya* male begot on a *vaiśya* woman (by the union) on the first day of the menses a caste *mahādasyu,* very strong and well-versed in archery. As he violated the words of his *kṣatriya* (father), he was declared to be *vāgatīta.*

119-120. *Mleccha* castes had their origin from a *kṣatriya* male and a *śūdra* woman (by the union) on the first day of the menses. They were dauntless and invincible on account of the sin. They had their ears not bored. They were cruel, fearless, invincible in battles, devoid of purificatory acts, dreadful and devoid of virtue.

121. The caste (called) *jola* had its origin from the *mleccha* male and *kuvinda* maiden. *Śarānka* is declared to be from Jola and *kuvinda maiden.*

122. On account of the defect of mixture of castes many unheard of castes (had come). O Brahmin! Who is capable of telling their names and numbers ?

123-124. *Vaidya* (physician) was born to Aśvinīkumāra begot on a brahmin maiden. Many men had their origin from *vaidya* male and *śūdra* woman. They were well-versed in folk arts and practitioners of mystic fomulae and herbs. Snake-charmers were born from them and *śūdra* woman.

Śaunaka said :

125. How did Aśvinīkumāra, the son of Sun god impregnate a *brāhmaṇa* spouse by imprudence?

Sauti said :

126. (Once) the passionate and tranquil Sun-god beheld a *brāhmaṇa* woman (proceeding) on pilgrimage in a lonely flower garden.

127. Although he was dissuaded by her, that mighty celestial beholding that beautiful lady forcibly impregnated her.

128. That lady discarded at once the foetus in that attractive flower garden. A son resembling the (colour of) heated gold came into being.

129. That ashamed lady took the child with her to her husband's place. She narrated her spouse the mishap that she has suffered on her way caused by the god.

130. The angry brahmin abandoned his spouse together with the son. On account of the virtue of her asceticism she became a river known as the Godāvarī.

131. The son of Sun-god himself taught his son with great effort the science of medical healing, different types of crafts and mystic formulae.

132. As that brahmin always made his subsistence by means of astrology, he became an astrologer discarded by the Vedic laws on the earth.

133. That greedy brahmin accepted gift in front of the *śūdras*. He became the first to accept the gifts made at the time of obsequial rites.

134. Certain person rose up from the sacrificial fire-pit in sacrificial rites. That Sūta (the bard), the exponent of dharma is known to be my predecessor.

135. (Lord) Brahmā, the mine of compassion, taught him the Purāṇas. Sūta who had his origin from the sacrificial pit (became) the reciter of the *purāṇas*.

136. A male was born from the Sūta and a *vaidya* woman. He was Bhaṭṭa, eloquent and singer of eulogies of all the people.

137. Thus I have explained you something about the mode of determining the castes on the earth. There are other innumerable castes on account of the mixture of castes.

138. I will explain you the relationship of the different persons (common to) all the different castes that has been told in the *vedas* and narrated by (Lord) Brahmā in the past.

139. The father (*pitā, tāta*) is known as the progenitor (*janaka, janmadātā*). One who gives birth to a child (jananī, *janayitrī* and *prasū*) is the mother (*ambā, mātā*).

140. Father's father is pitāmaha (grandfather). The father of the latter is *prapitāmaha* (great grand father). The later descendants are known to be sagotra (belonging to the same class).

141. The father of the mother is known as mātāmaha (maternal grandfather). The progenitor of the mātāmaha is

pramātāmaha (great grandfather). The latter's father is great great (grandfather).

142. The mother of the father is *pitāmahi* (grandmother). Her mother-in-law is *prapitāmahi*. Her mother-in-law is known as *vṛddhaprapitāmahi* (great great grandmother).

143. The mother of the mother is *mātāmahī* (grandmother). She is regarded similar to the mother. The spouse of the *pramātāmaha* (great maternal grandfather) is known as *pramātāmaha* (great maternal grandmother).

144. The spouse of the father of *pramātāmaha* is known as *vṛddhamātāmahi* (great great maternal grandmother). The brother of the father is *pitṛvya* (paternal uncle). The brother of the mother is *mātula* (maternal uncle).

145. The sister of the father is *pitṛṣvasā* and the sister of the mother is known as *mātṛṣvasā*. The son is known as *tanaya* (born from the body), *putra*, *dāyāda* (entitled to a share in ancestral property), *ātmeja* (born from one's own self).

146. The recipient of wealth and born of the semen virile are (used to denote) a male offspring. A female descendant is (denoted by the words) *duhitā*, *kanyā* and *ātmajā* (born of the self).

147. The wife of the son is known to be *vadhū* (daughter-in-law). The husband of the daughter is *jāmātā* (son-in-law). The terms denoting a husband are : *pati*, *priya*(dear), *bhartā*(supporter), svāmi, (master) and *kānta* (lover).

148. The brother of the husband is devara (brother-in-law). The sister of the brother is *nanāndā* (sister-in-law). *Śvaśura* (father-in-law) is the father of the husband. *Śvaśrū* (mother-in-law) is the mother of the husband.

149. The wife is known as *bhāryā*, *jāyā*, *priyā*, *kāntā* and strī. The brother of the wife is *śyālaka*. The sister of the wife is *śyālikā*.

150. The mother of the wife is *śvaśū*. The father of the wife is known as *śvaśuraḥ*. One who is born from the same womb is *sodara*, *bhrātā* (brother). A girl born together is *bhaginī* (sister).

151. The son of the sister is *bhāgineya* and the son of the brother is *bhrātṛja*. The husband of the sister is *ārutta*, *bhaginīkānta* and *bhaginīpati*.

152. The husband of wife's sister is a brother for the reason that the father-in-law is the same. O sage ! The father-in-law is to be known as the father. He is equal to one's own father.

153. Giver of food, protector from danger, father of the wife, giver of knowledge and progenitor are the five fathers of men.

154-155. The fourteen mothers are the wife of the giver of good, the sister, the wife of the preceptor, the mother, the step-mother, the daughter, the spouse of the son, the mother of the mother, the mother of the father, the mother-in-law, the sister of the father, the wife of the paternal uncle and the wife of the maternal uncle.

156. The son's son is stated to be a *pautra* (grandson), his son is *prapautra* (great grandson). His sons and others of the same lineage (are stated to be) *kulajāḥ* (born in the same family).

157. The son of the daughter is *dauhitra* (grandson). Her descendants (are) kinsmen. The sons and others (relatives) of the sister are known to be kinsmen.

158. The sons and descendants of the son of the brother are known to be *jñātis* (agnate relatives). The son, the brother and the dependent of the preceptor are dear kinsmen.

159. O Sage ! The daughter of the preceptor, (his) sister and female dependents (are to be regarded) as equal to the mother. The preceptor of the son, the brother (of the preceptor) and the dependents are very intimate kinsmen.

160. The father-in-law of the son (is) a brother and is known to be a matrimonial kinsman. A similar relationship is stated to be for the father-in-law of the daughter.

161. The preceptor of one's sister (is) a brother and an intimate kinsman. The preceptor of the father-in-law and brothers are stated to be equivalent to the preceptor.

162. One is stated to be a friend with whom there is good relationship. A friend is known to be yielding happiness. One that causes grief is stated to be an enemy.

163. By providence a kinsman (becomes) a conferer of grief and a person not having any association (becomes) a conferer of unhappiness. O foremost Brahmin ! There are three types of associations for men on the earth.

164. They are stated to be from learning, from common uterus, and from satisfaction. A friend is to be known as causing satisfaction. That association is very difficult (to find).

165. The mother of the friend and the wife of the friend are no doubt equal to one's mother. The brother of a friend and the father of a friend are respectively equal to the brother and father of men.

166. The Lotus-born (Brahmā) stated that the fourth (relationship) is nominal relationship. The person copulating with an unchaste woman is a paramour (*jāra, upapati*) and a relative.

167-170. The mistress is (known as) *navajñā, preyasī* (beloved) and *cittahāriṇī* (fascinating). The paramour is equal to the husband. *Navajñā* is equal to the house-wife. This relationship (is correct) in a different region only and condemned in all the regions. It is not in the *vedas* and much censured. It has been instituted by (sage) Viśvāmitra. As this custom cannot be dispensed with even by great people it has been practised in a different region. It is scandalous for men and especially for women. As it is prevalent in different *yugas* it will not be a blemish for glorious people.

CHAPTER ELEVEN

The Greatness of a Devotee of Viṣṇu

Śaunaka said :

1. After forsaking his wife what did the brahmin do ? O Fortunate one ! Who were the Aśvins ? In whose family were they born ?

Sauti said :

2. That brahmin named Sutapā, a great sage, belonging to the family of (sage) Bharadvāja, did penance for a lac years in the Himālayas (contemplating) (Lord) Kṛṣṇa.

3. That glorious great ascetic glowing with the *brāhmaṇa* radiance suddenly beheld the lustre of Lord (Kṛṣṇa) for a while in the sky.

4. (Finding) himself untainted and above the nature, he did not seek for liberation. He begged for unswerving devotion and servitude.

5. Then there was a voice in the heaven asking him to get married assuring servitude later and devotion after the enjoyment ceases.

6-7. (Lord) Brahmā himself presented him the mental daughter of the manes. O Foremost sage! Kalyāṇamitra was born to her, by the mere remembrance of whose name there will not be any fear from thunder.[1] The mere remembrance of his name would secure back the lost articles and friends.

8-9. After having abandoned the mother of Kalyāṇamitra, the great sage cursed the son of Sun-god: O Basest among gods ! You would be deprived of the share in the sacrificial rites. Along with your brother you will not be worshipped (now onwards). You will be diseased and paralysed and deprived of celebrity.

10. After having cursed thus, Sutapā left for his house along with his son. Sun-god approached him with the Aśvins.

11. O Śaunaka ! Sun-god, the Lord of the three worlds, accompanied by his diseased sons eulogised Sutapā, the foremost sage.

Sun-god said :

12. O Venerable brahmin ! A form of Viṣṇu in the different *yugas* ! Descendant of Bharadvāja! Foremost ascetic ! Forgive the offence done by my son.

13. Brahmā, Viṣṇu, Maheśa and all other gods always partake the fruits, flowers, water etc., offered by a brahmin.

14. The gods invoked by the brahmins are always worshipped in the world. There is no god superior to a brahmin. Lord Hari (Viṣṇu) (takes) the form of a brahmin.

15. When a brahmin gets pleased, (Lord) Nārāyaṇa himself gets pleased. When (Lord) Nārāyaṇa gets pleased, all the other gods get pleased.

16. There is no sacred place equal to the Ganges. There is no god superior to (Lord) Kṛṣṇa. There is no devotee of (Lord) Viṣṇu (equal to Lord) Śaṅkara. There is no one more enduring than the earth.

17. There is no virtue superior to truth. There is no pious lady superior to (goddess) Pārvatī. No one is stronger than fate. There is no one dearer than the son.

18. There is no enemy equal to a disease. There is no one more respectable than the preceptor. There is no kinsman equal to one's mother. There is no friend superior to one's father.

19. Nothing (is superior) to the austerity of *ekādaśi*[2] (the eleventh day). There is nothing superior to fasting. There is no wealth superior to the gems. Knowledge is a gem superior to that.

20. A brahmin is superior in all the stages of life. The Lotus-born (Brahmā) has declared that there is no preceptor equal to a brahmin well-versed with the import of the *vedas* and *vedāṅgas*.

21. After listening to the words of the Sun-god, the descendent of Bharadvāja bowed to him.

22-23. After having told him that the two sons would later become recipients of the shares of sacrificial offerings, the sage Sutapā bowed to Sun-god and hastened to the Ganges bent on worshipping (Lord) Hari. The Sun-god proceeded to His abode along with His sons.

24. By the blessings of the brahmin those two became adorable and recipients of the shares of sacrificial offerings. Whoever reads this eulogy on the brahmin made by the Sun-god, he would be victorious everywhere by the grace of the feet of the brahmin.

25. Getting up in the morning, whoever reads 'Salutations to the brahmins', he (would get the merits) of bathing in all the sacred waters and get initiated in all the sacrifices.

26. All the sacred waters on the earth (are present) in the ocean. All the waters present in the ocean (are present) in the feet of the brahmins.

27. As long as the earth gets moistened with the water (that has washed) the feet of a brahmin, till then the manes drink the water from the lotus cups.

28. Whoever drinks with devotion the meritorious water (that has washed) the feet of a brahmin, he would be (deemed to have) bathed in all the sacred waters and initiated in all the sacrifices.

29. O Brahmin ! If a person having a great disease drinks the water (that has washed) the feet of a brahmin for a month with devotion, he becomes free from all diseases.

30. Whether one is ignorant or learned, if a brahmin has been purified by (the performance of) twilight worship, he himself is deemed to be equal to (Lord) Viṣṇu, if he has no aversion for (Lord) Viṣṇu.

31. An assaulting or cursing brahmin should not be assaulted or cursed. A brahmin devoted to (Lord) Viṣṇu is hundred times more venerable than the cows.

32. O Brahmin ! Whoever partakes the water (used for washing) the feet of a brahmin and offering made to a brahmin (he is a devotee of Viṣṇu). Whoever partakes daily the offering (made to a brahmin), gains the fruit of the *rājasūya*[3] (sacrifice).

33. A place certainly becomes a sacred place after getting the water used for (washing) the feet of a brahmin who does not eat on the *ekādaśī* (eleventh day) and worships (Lord) Kṛṣṇa daily.

34. Whoever partakes daily the remnants of food offered to Lord Kṛṣṇa, he (becomes) purified and liberated while living on the earth.

35. (Lord) Brahmā told that the food and milk (in the house) of a brahmin born in a good family not offered to (Lord) Viṣṇu (are) ordure and urine (respectively).

36. (Lord) Brahmā and sons of Brahmā and all are devoted to (Lord) Viṣṇu. How could a brahmin born in that family be averse to (Lord) Hari?

37. The brahmins who are averse to (Lord) Kṛṣṇa on account of the fault of the association of the parents, maternal grandfather and the preceptor and others, are dead even while leaving.

38. Whoever does not turn his mind towards (Lord) Hari is a bad preceptor, bad father, bad son, bad friend, bad king and bad kinsman.

39. O Brahmin ! A *caṇḍāla* devotee of (Lord) Viṣṇu is better than a brahmin not devoted to (Lord) Viṣṇu. (While that) low-born person gets liberated together with his attendants, the brahmin goes to hell.

40. (A brahmin) without (offering) the daily worship or a brahmin averse towards (Lord) Kṛṣṇa is impure. Just as a serpent devoid of poison, he is a semblance of a brahmin.

41. (Lord) Brahmā would state that such a person is a devotee of Viṣṇu, very much purified and liberated while living, in whose ear enters the mystic formula, namely, (Lord) Viṣṇu, from the mouth of the preceptor.

42. A devotee of (Lord) Viṣṇu would go to the place of (Lord) Hari along with hundreds of maternal grandfathers and crore of men belonging to his family.

43. Just as these are the four castes such as the brahmin, warrior, tradesmen and *śudras,* there is an independent caste in this world known as the *vaiṣṇava* (devotee of Viṣṇu).

44-45. The devotees of (Lord) Viṣṇu contemplate the lotus feet of (Lord) Govinda. (Lord) Govinda also contemplates them always in their presence deputing (his weapon) *sudarśana* (wheel) for the protection of his devotees. Even then he never remains without any anxiety in their presence.

CHAPTER TWELVE

The Birth of Nārada as a *Gandharva*

Śaunaka said:

1. Although I have not raised it myself, I have heard with curiosity the different legends incidentally with (the narration of) the genealogy of sages.

2-3. Who all carried on creation? Who all remained celibates? What did Nārada do after quarrelling with his father ? What did happen to the son on account of the curse of the father after the quarrel ? (What happened) to the father on account of the curse of the son? O Sauti ! Narrate me that auspicious one.

Sauti said :

4-5. O Śaunaka ! Except Haṁsa, Yati, Araṇi, Voḍhu, Pañcaśikha, Apāntaratamas and Sanaka and others, many other sons of Brahmā were ever householders and had children obeying the command of the preceptor.

6. The progenitor Brahmā himself was not being worshipped on account of the curse of the son. It is only hence the learned people do not worship (repeat) the mystic formula of (Lord) Brahmā.

7. On account of the curse of the preceptor (Brahmā), Nārada became a *gandharva.* You listen to my narration of that extensive story.

8-9. A foremost *gandharva* king of all the *gandharvas,* endowed with all prosperity, but not having progeny on account of his (past) action feeling grief-stricken and put down in spirit performed a penance at Puṣkara with steadfast meditation on Śambhu at the command of his preceptor.

10. (Sage) Vasiṣṭha, the mine of compassion, gave the king of *gandharvas* an amulet, hymn and mystic syllable of (Lord) Śiva.

11. O Sage ! Being tormented by the grief of not having a child, he repeated the excellent divine formula for hundred years abstaining from food.

12-18. At the end of hundred years, he beheld (Lord) Śiva in front of him: lighting up the ten directions shining with *brahmin* lustre, having a form of great radiance–a blessed one, eternal, having a mild smile, having a pleasant face, doing favour to the devotees,– a form of penance, seed of penance, conferer of the fruits of penance, bestower of all prosperity on the devotee seeking refuge, bearing the trident and *paṭṭiśa*(a kind of spear), seated on the bull, nude, having the complexion of pure crystal, three-eyed, bearing the crescent on the head, bearing the excellent knotty tuft excelling the lustre of heated gold,— having a blue throat, omniscient, having the serpent as the sacred thread, destroyer of all, time personified, the conqueror of (god of) death, shining with the lustre of a crore of mid-day sun of the summer, the suzerain lord, conferer of the knowledge about the reality, tranquil, bestower of liberation and giver of devotion to (Lord) Viṣṇu. That *gandharva* at once prostrated flat like a staff on the earth.

19. He eulogised the Supreme Lord with the hymn given to him by (sage) Vasiṣṭha. (Lord) Śiva, the mine of compassion, asked him to seek a boon. He sought (the favour of) devotion to (Lord) Hari and a son extremely devoted to (Lord) Viṣṇu.

20. After listening to the words of the Gandharva, the Lord of the indigent and a friend of the poor, (Lord) Candraśekhara (Śiva, having the moon on the head), spoke to him.

Śrī Mahādeva said :

21. By your first boon you must have got satisfied. But your second request is merely a repetition. O King of the *gandharvas* ! No one is easily satisfied with the good things in the world.

22. O Child ! Whoever has firm and most auspicious devotion to (Lord) Hari, he is capable of protecting the entire universe sportively.

23. Certainly he goes to the Goloka elevating a crore of people of his family and a hundred of his maternal grandfather.

24. After destroying the three kinds of sins acquired in crore births he would enjoy merits and certainly become a servant of (Lord) Hari.

25. So long as (Lord) Kṛṣṇa (dwells) in one's mind, last one's wife, son, cherished property, happiness and grief.

26. When (Lord) Kṛṣṇa gets fixed in one's mind, the sword, namely, the devotion that is hard to be attained, cuts asunder at the root of the tree of (past) actions of men.

27. The virtuous ones, to whom sons extremely devoted to (Lord) Viṣṇu are born, they, sportively elevate crore of their family.

28. A seeker of boons accomplishes the desired object by a single boon. What is the need for the second boon ? There is no satisfaction (even after gaining) the auspicious one.

29. Devotion and service to (Lord) Kṛṣṇa, that is most difficult (to be gained) by the devotion of (Lord) Viṣṇu, and which is our acquired wealth, we are not interested in giving it way.

30. O Child! You ask some other boon that you wish in your mind. You attain the positions of Indra, gods or Brahmā.

31. I shall bestow on you with ease all accomplishments, great asceticism, knowledge and conquest over death etc. But you relinquish (the request for) service to (Lord) Hari.

32. After listening to the words of (Lord) Śaṅkara, the indigent (*gandharva*) with parched throat, lips and palate, spoke to the friend of the poor and conferer of all prosperities.

The gandharva said :

33. A devotee of (Lord) Kṛṣṇa would not aspire for the dream-like position of Brahmā which would crumble down by the mere winking of the eyelid.

34. O Śiva ! A devotee (of Kṛṣṇa) would not aspire for the positions of Indra and gods, accomplishments, asceticism etc., knowledge, or conquest over death etc.

35-36. The devotees of (Lord) Viṣṇu would not aspire for residence in the same world, holding the same power, nearness or intimate union with Lord Hari or final liberation because it will be very difficult to have firm devotion or service to (Lord) Hari therein for ever. The devotees seek this foremost boon either in dream or while awake.

37. O wish-yielding tree ! Grant me that service and an excellent son devoted to (Lord) Viṣṇu. The meanest gets all the boons by approaching you, the foremost one and (becomes) satisfied.

38. O Śambhu! If you do not grant this boon to me, a sinner, I will cut off my head and offer it to fire.

39. After listening to the words of the *gandharva*, that mine of compassion, the master of the devotees and the gracious on the devotees spoke to that indigent devotee.

40-41. You obtain this boon from me to have devotion and service to (Lord) Hari and a son. He would be much devoted to Viṣṇu, long living, virtuous, having eternal youth, wise, most handsome, devoted to the preceptor, one who has subdued the senses and one who is the foremost king of the Gandharvas. You need not have any grief. aspire for residence in the same world, holding the same power, nearness or intimate union with Lord Hari or final liberartion because it will be very difficult to have firm devotion or service to (Lord) Hari therein for ever. The devotees seek this foremost boon either in dream or while awake.

37. O Wish-yielding tree ! Grant me that service and an excellent son devoted to (Lord) Viṣṇu. The meanest gets all the boons by approaching you, the foremost one and (becomes) satisfied.

38. O Śambhu ! If you do not grant this boon to me, a sinner, I will cut off my head and offer it to fire.

39. After listening to the words of the Gandharva, that mine of compassion, the master of the devotees and the gracious on the devotees spoke to that indigent devotee.

Śrī Śaṅkara said :

40-41. You obtain this boon from me to have devotion and service to (Lord) Hari and a son.

42. O Sage ! After having spoken thus, (Lord) Śaṅkara went back to his place. The *gandharva* king felt pleased and came back to his mansion.

43. All the men felt delighted that the task was accomplished. (Sage) Nārada was born to his wife in Bhārata.

44-45. That old lady delivered the son on the Gandhamādana mountain. The venerable preceptor (sage) Vasiṣṭha gave that boy a suitable and auspicious name on an auspicious day. The term '*upa*' has the sense of 'more' and '*barhaṇa*' (the sense of) adorable. As he was most adorable, that boy was christened as '*upabarhaṇa*'.

CHAPTER THIRTEEN

The Lamentation of Mālāvatī, a *Gandharva* Woman

Sauti said :

1. With great rejoice that king of the *gandharvas* gifted different kinds of gems and riches to the brahmins.

2. Upabarhaṇa obtained the most difficult formula relating to (Lord) Hari duly from (sage) Vasiṣṭha and then performed an arduous penance.

3. Once the wives of the *gandharvas* beheld his handsome form on the banks of the Gaṇḍakī river and fell into a swoon at once.

4. They did intense penance and discarded their lives by ascetic practices. They then became the fifty daughters of Citraratha.

5. They chose the *gandharva* Upabarhaṇa as their husband. Those libidinous women gladly gave him a garland at the command of their father.

6. That perennially youthful *gandharva* accepted them. That lustful person indulged in making merry with them in solitude for three lacs of years.

7. After that he ruled the kingdom for a long time always in their company. O Sage ! Then he came to the place of (Lord) Brahmā singing the eulogy on (Lord) Hari.

8. He then beheld the beautiful Rambhā with her robust breast dancing there. Then there was the discharge (of semen) from that great *gandharva.*

9. Immediately he ceased to sing and fell into a swoon in the assembly. The gods burst into a fit of laughter. (Lord) Brahmā angrily cursed him—

10. You discard the form of a *gandharva* and take to the womb of a *śudra.* In course of time you will become my son on account of the association with the devotees of (Lord) Viṣṇu.

11. O Son ! There will never be greatness for men without adversity. There will be happiness and grief for all people by turns.

12. After having spoken thus, (Lord) Brahmā went to his abode in Puṣkara. The *gandharva* Upabarhaṇa also discarded his body then.

13-18a. After having pierced the six (mystic circles known as the *mūlādhāra, svādhiṣṭhāna, maṇipūra, anāhata, viśuddha* and *ājñā*[1] and penetrated the sixteen arteries: *iḍā, suṣumnā, medhā, piṅgalā, pr āṇahāsiṇī, sarvajñānapradā, manassaṁyaminī, viśuddhā, niruddhā, vāyusañcāriṇī, tejaśśukakarī, balapuṣṭikarī, buddhisañcāriṇī, jñānajṛmbhhanakāriṇī, sarvaprāṇaharā* and *punarjivanakāriṇī,* he brought the sentient soul together with his mind to the *brahmarandra* (the aperture at the top of the head) by means of meditation. After having remained in that state for a while, he united that in his own self.

18b-21. O Śaunaka ! Then that foremost ascetic remembered his past birth and realised brahman after having placed the rare to get three-stringed lute on his left shoulder and holding a pure crystal garland in his right hand and repeating the two syllables 'Kṛṣṇa', that is the Supreme Brahman, the essence of the *vedas,* most supreme, and the excellent germ of redemption and lying down just as a person on a bed of *darbha* (grass) with his head placed on the east and the pair of feet in the west.

22. In the company of his wife the *gandharva* king beheld him and attained brahman by meditation after having mentally contemplated Śrī Kṛṣṇa.

23. All the wives and kinsmen of the king lamented and wept aloud. Being tormented by grief they all fell into a swoon in course of time due to the illusion of (Lord) Viṣṇu.

24-25. The chief queen among the fifty wives, Mālāvatī by name, pious, outstanding and extremely dear, embracing her husband and weeping aloud with intense grief uttered the following words addressing her spouse.

Mālāvatī said :

26. O Lord ! Excellent husband! Clever one! The foremost connoisseur! Kinsman! Become visible to me drowned in the ocean of grief.

27-31. My mind is afflicted by the sport you had with this wretched self in solitude in the spring (season) in the past in a confidential abode in the beautiful sandal forest, in an attractive flower garden on the banks of the Puṣpabhadrā river, in the charming sandal forest in the vicinity of Candana mountain, on the bed of flowers and sandal made fragrant by the breeze (carrying the fragrance of) the sandal, on a spot on the Gandhamādana mountain on the charming banks of a river, resplendent with the mass of Mālatī (shrubs) resounding with the notes of the male cuckoos, in the divine forest on the *śrīśaila* frequented by (Lord) Śrīnivāsa (Lord Viṣṇu having goddess Lakṣmī on the chest), consecrated by the footsteps of (goddess) Lakṣmī and visited by (Lord) Acyuta (Viṣṇu).

32. I have been drenched by your nectar-like words in the past. I am always tormented very cruelly by (the remembrance of) those words.

33. Association with a virtuous person is more difficult to be gained than the Vaikuṇṭha. The long separation is more difficult to tide over than even the death (of the self).

34. Hence the separation from them makes the virtuous feel more anguish. Then the grief arising from the separation of the kinsman is very cruelsome.

35. Then the separation from the progeny surpasses (the grief) of death. The separation from one's husband is above all. There is no mishap superior to it.

36. The grief (arising) from the separation from one's husband gets renewed everyday while sleeping, eating, bathing, sleeping and waking.

37. A lady is able to forget all her grief by the mere association of her husband. I do not find any other kinsman on seeing whom one may forget the husband.

38. Hence I do not find an outstanding kinsman excelling the husband for virtuous women born in a good family. Thus the Lotus-born (Brahmā) has said.

39. O Regents of the quarters ! Guardians of the quarters! (Lord) of Virtue ! O Brahmā ! O Lord of mountains (Śiva) ! O Consort of Kamalā (Viṣṇu) ! Grant me the gift of my husband.

40. Having spoken thus, that daughter of Citraratha tormented by separation, fell into a swoon there getting itself in that inaccessible dense forest.

41. Having placed her husband on the chest, she remained there unconscious for a whole day and night being protected by all the gods.

42. Having gained her consciousness in the morning, she lamented very much again. That chaste woman spoke again addressing (Lord) Hari.

Mālāvatī said:

43. O (Lord) Kṛṣṇa ! Lord of the world ! O Lord! I am not outside the world! You are the protector of the world. O Lord! How is it that you are not protecting me ?

44. This (is my) husband. I (am his) wife. I, mine all these things are due to your illusion. In fact you are the sole master and sole cause of everything.

45. By virtue of his action, the *gandharva* (has become) my husband and I (have become) his wife on account of his action. Where has he gone after enjoying (the fruits of) his action after leaving me his dear wife ?

46. O Lord ! Who is one's husband or son ? Or who is whose wife ? (Lord) Brahmā writes and separates them by their action.

47. Always there is great rejoice in union and mortal agony in separation for the ignorant in the world but certainly not for a person delighting in one's self.

48. Truly, all the matter, the pleasures on the world and kinsmen are transient. One who renounces on his own feels pleasure. But one who is made to renounce feels pain.

49. Hence the virtuous people renouncing on their own all the desired prosperity, meditate always the trouble-free lotus feet of (Lord) Kṛṣṇa.

50. Only virtuous men are always wise. But which lady is wise in the world ? Hence it is proper on your part to grant me, the ignorant one, the desired one.

51. I do not desire to be immortal. Nor do I aspire for the position of Indra, nor the path of liberation. Grant me my husband that confers the supreme four-fold (goals of human existence).

52. O Lord of the universe ! No woman in this world ever obtained a husband like mine from (Lord) Brahmā.

53. O Hari ! He was endowed with all the qualities, different forms and all good conducts except being immortal.

54. My Lord was equal to (Lord) Hari by his form, quality, lustre, valour, knowledge, tranquility and contentment.

55-59. (He was) a devotee of (Lord) Hari and hence he was equal to (Lord) Hari. He was deep like the ocean, radiant like the Sun, pure like the fire, good-looking like the moon, handsome like the god of love, having an intellect like Bṛhaspati and having poetical skill like Kāvya (Śukra). He was well-versed in all the branches of learning like (goddess) Vāṇī (Sarasvatī). In his genius he resembled Bhṛgu. He was wealthy equal to Kubera (Lord of wealth). He was munificient like

Manu. He was virtuous like Dharma in virtue. He excelled Satyavrata in truth. He was like Kumāra (Sanatkumāra) in ascetic practices. He equalled (Lord) Brahmā in his religious practices. He was equal to Indra in sovereignty. He resembled the earth in forbearance. Such a type of my husband is dead. How is it that I am not dead ?

60. O Gods ! As recipients of a share of the sacrificial offerings on earth you are eligible to partake the ghee. In a trice I will sportively deprive you of your right for sacrificial offerings.

61. O Nārāyaṇa ! Lord of the World ! I alone am not outside the world. Quickly revive my husband, otherwise I will curse you.

62. O Brahmā ! You are (already) not fit for worship on earth on account of the curse of your son. Now I will deprive you of your privilege of authority over mundane existence.

63. O Śambhu (Śiva)! I will curse you to lose knowledge. Sportively I will deprive Dharma of his virtue.

64. No doubt, I will drive away the authority of Yama. I will curse Truth and Time and Suniṣṭhurā, the daughter of Death.

65. I will curse everyone now here itself except decrepitude and disease because my husband did not die on account of sickness or old age.

66. After having spoken thus, the most pious lady Mālāvatī, holding the corpse on her chest, came to the banks of (the river) Kauśikī, in order to curse them.

67. Seeing her about to curse them, (Lord) Brahmā leading the other gods, sought the refuge of (Lord) Viṣṇu on the banks of the milky ocean.

68. After bathing there he eulogised the Supreme Lord. (Lord) Brahmā, becoming frightened spoke to (Lord) Viṣṇu, the Lord of the world thus.

Brahmā said :

69. That daughter of Citraratha and wife of Upabarhaṇa may curse me and the gods for (the loss of) her husband. O Mādhava (Consort of Lakṣmī) ! You protect us.

70. The pious and virtuous remember Mādhava. The ascetics happily repeat (the name) in their dreams and while awake and in all their actions.

71. (Lord) Hṛṣīkeśa (Viṣṇu) ! One bent on protecting the indigent seeking refuge! Save us! We seek your refuge.

72. O Lord! My worship has been impeded now on account of the curse of my son. The chaste Mālatī is now depriving me of my authority.

73. O Lord ! You have vested me with all the authority over the Brahmāṇḍa in the past. O Lord ! All such prosperity belonging to me will be lost now.

Mahādeva said :

74. Great, secret and rare wisdom has been granted to me at Puṣkara in the past as a fruit of my penance for hundred *manvantara* (periods).

75. Prosperity or wealth or knowledge or valour does not deserve to be equal to a sixteenth part of that supreme wisdom.

76. My excellent true wisdom, not known by all, secret and very difficult to get is to be lost on account of the curse of that woman.

77. Ah ! The splendour of a chaste lady is above the splendour of all. O Hari ! Protect my burn from that fire of lustre.

Dharma said :

78. Virtue is eternal and is the foremost among all jewels. O Lord ! Such a virtue conferred by you in the past will go away.

79. O Supreme Lord ! The virtue obtained as a fruit of penance for seven *manvantara* periods is being lost view on account of the curse of the woman.

The Gods said :

80. O Mādhava ! You have made us recipient of the offerings of ghee at the sacrifices. All that will be lost now on account of the curse of that woman.

81. After having stated thus, all of them subdued and frightened stood there. In the meanwhile, accidentally there was an invisible voice.

82. O Gods ! You go to her. Janārdana in the guise of a brahmin would go there later for the sake of peace and for your protection.

83. After hearing those words, the gods went to the place of Mālāvatī on the banks of (the river) Kauśikī with delighted mind.

84-91. The gods beheld the chaste and divine Mālāvatī resplendent with ornaments of exquisite gems. She had the beauty of the goddess of wealth. She was wearing an apparel pure as the fire. She was adorned with a vermilion dot. She had the lustre of the autumnal moon. She was calm. By her splendour she was lighting up the quarters. The lustre that she had amassed by the great virtue of serving her husband was making her radiant like an excellent glowing fire-brand. Holding the corpse on her chest she was seated in a meditative posture. She was holding the beautiful lute of her husband in her right hand.She was holding with devotion and affection the pure crystal garland of her spouse with the tips of her forefinger and thumb in *yogamudrā*.[2] Her complexion was that of charming *campaka* (flowers). She had red lips. She was wearing a garland of gems. She had the perennial youth as that of a sixteen year old (girl). She was afflicted by the weight of stout rump. She had plumpy loins and breasts. She was again and again looking at the corpse of her Lord with auspicious look. Beholding her in such a state, those gods were surprised. The virtuous ones being afraid of righteousness stood dumbfounded for a while.

CHAPTER FOURTEEN

The Dialogue between Mālāvatī and Viṣṇu and the Greatness of Kṛṣṇa

Sauti said :

1. The most benevolent gods lead by Brahmā and Īśāna stood there for a while and went near Mālāvatī.

2. O Sage ! Beholding the gods, the chaste Mālāvatī saluted them and after placing (the body of) her husband in front of the gods, she wept.

3. In the meanwhile, a very handsome brahmin boy arrived in the midst of the assembly of gods.

4-6. He was holding a staff and umbrella. He was wearing a white dress. He had a sparkling mark (on the forehead). He was having a long book in his hand. He was very much calm. He was smiling. He had besmeared sandal (paste) all over his limbs. He was shining with the lustre of brahman. After having conversed with the surprised gods there, by the spell of Viṣṇu he sat in the midst of the gods like the moon in the midst of the stars. That wise one then spoke to the gods and Mālatī (Mālāvatī).

The Brahmin said:

7-9. Why have the gods followed by Brahmā and Īśāna come here ? What is the cause of Brahmā becoming the creator of the world ? How is Lord Śambhu (Śiva) the destroyer of all the Brahmāṇḍa ? How is (Lord) Dharma the witness of all the actions of the three world ? Why Sun, Moon, Fire-god, Kāla, the daughter of God of Death, Yama and others have come here ?

10. O Mālāvatī ! Sinless one ! What is the dry dead body on your lap ? How is the corpse of a male on the lap of the living woman ?

11. After having told her thus, the brahmin stopped talking in the assembly. Mālāvatī bowed and replied that wise man.

Mālāvatī said :

12. I salute (Lord) Janārdana, in the form of a brahmin, with pleasure. If (Lord) Hari is pleased, the gods get pleased with the flower water offered to Him.

13. O Lord ! You consider carefully the submission of the grief-stricken one. Pious people have always the same compassion towards the deserving and non-deserving.

14. I am the daughter of Citraratha and the wife of Upabarhaṇa. O Foremost brahmin ! All the people call me Mālāvatī.

15. I was amusing at my sweet-will in the charming places all around with my husband for a divine lakh of yugas.

16. O Wise one! Foremost Brahmin ! You know the extent of affection that the chaste women have for their husbands according to the treatises.

17. My husband lost his life on account of the curse of (Lord) Brahmā without any reason. I lamented before the gods for the revival of my husband.

18. But all (people) in the world are engaged in accomplishing their selfish aims. They do not know the feelings (of others). They are bent on their selfish goals.

19. Happiness, unhappiness, fear, grief, distress, prosperity, supreme pleasure, birth, death and liberation are due to the acts of men.

20. The gods are the cause for everything. They are the bestowers of fruits for the actions (of men). They cut asunder at the roots of the trees of actions by sportive gesture.

21. There is no greater relative than the gods. There is no one stronger than the gods. There is no one more compassionate or a greater bestower than the gods.

22. I seek the most favourite of mine, namely, the gift of (my) husband from the gods who are the celestial trees conferring the fruits of *dharma* (virtue), *artha*(prosperity) *kāma* (pleasure) and *mokṣa* (liberation).

23. It is better if the gods restore me my husband as desired by me. Otherwise I will certainly curse them to be the cause for killing a woman.

24. I shall inflict a dreadful and irrevocable curse on all of them. The curse of a chaste woman is irrevocable by means of penance or any other means.

25. O Śaunaka ! After having spoken thus in the assembly of the gods, the pious Mālatī (Mālāvatī), overwhelmed with grief, gave a pause. The foremost brahmin replied her.

The Brahmin said:

26. O Mālatī ! It is true that the gods are the bestowers of fruits of the actions. Just as the farmer cannot reap the grains at once and have to wait for a long time, so also in the case of men.

27. When the householder sows the grain in the field through the farmer, that sprout grows into a tree in course of time and bears fruits.

28. In due course it becomes ripe and the householder reaps the benefit after sometime. In this way all the fruits of the actions have to be reaped.

29. The householder sows the seed in mundane existence by means of the illusion of (Lord) Viṣṇu. It sprouts in course of time and becomes a tree later. In due course one reaps the fruit.

30. A meritorious one performs a penance for a long time in a sacred place. There is no doubt that the gods are truly the conferrers of fruits.

31. Whatever one offers with devotion to the mouth of a brahmin, an excellent field and not a desert, that he certainly reaps.

32. Without penance (one cannot get) strength, beauty, prosperity, wealth, progeny, wife and husband.

33. One who serves the *prakṛti*(Primordial Nature) with devotion would get a beautiful and modest wife endowed with qualities in every birth.

34. A devotee would get permanent wealth, son, grandson, land, riches and progeny by the favour of *prakṛti,* as a sport.

35-36. Whoever worships in every birth with devotion Lord Śiva, the embodiment of auspiciousness, conferrer of good, cause of good, bliss of wisdom, great soul and the foremost conqueror of death, would get a good wife, if he is a male and a good husband, if she is a female.

37. By the grace of (Lord) Hara (Śiva) one would get knowledge, wisdom, poetic skill, son, grandson, opulence, strength, wealth and valour.

38. One who worships (Lord) Brahmā, would also get progeny, wealth, knowledge, prosperity and happiness by the favour of (Lord) Brahmā.

39. Whoever worships (Lord) Sun, the Lord of the indigent, would certainly get knowledge, good health, happiness, wealth and sons.

40-41. Whoever worships with devotion in every birth, the Lord of the gaṇas, the Lord of Lords, eternal one, the first worshipped among all and the Lord of all beings, his obstacles would be destroyed in the dream and in the waking state. He would get supreme happiness, prosperity, son, grandson, wealth and progeny.

42-45. One would get wisdom, knowledge and good poetic skill by his favour. Whoever worships (Lord) Viṣṇu, the consort of Lakṣmī and the Lord of the gods, would certainly get everything if he is a seeker of favour, or liberation if otherwise. By worshipping that tranquil protector, a man would certainly get, all penance, all virtues, fame and outstanding glory. One who worships (Lord) Viṣṇu, the Lord of all the beings and seeks a favour, that ignorant person would be deceived by (Lord) Brahmā, being deluded by the illusion of (Lord Viṣṇu). The illusion of (Lord) Nārāyaṇa is the governess holding her sway over all nature.

46. She confers the mystic formula of (Lord) Viṣṇu on those towards whom she is compassionate. The virtuous one doing pious deeds would certainly gain all virtues.

47-48a. After enjoying happiness in this world, one would attain the excellent place of (Lord) Viṣṇu. One would attain first that position of that Lord whom he worships. In course of time he would reach the position of (Lord) Viṣṇu along with him (the god whom he worships first).

48b-51. Whoever worships (Lord) Śrī Kṛṣṇa without quality, transcending nature, adored by (Lord) Brahmā, Viṣṇu and Śiva and others, the seed, transcending the supreme, without decay, Supreme Brahman, the venerable one, the eternal one, endowed with form, without a form, lustre, the Lord who is an embodiment of free-will, support of all the beings, Lord of all the beings, Supreme bliss, the Suzerain Lord, unstained, of the form of a witness, an embodied one conferring favour on the devotees, such a person is truly a liberated one while living, if that good person does not seek any favour.

52-54. Such a person would consider the four states such as being in the same world as the Lord etc., as a chaff. The positions of Brahmā or the gods or liberation are worthless for him. Wealth is equal to a lump of earth for him. He regards it as perishable. He counts the positions of Indra or Manu and immortality as a bubble of water and as extremely worthless. He desires always to serve (the Lord) in his dream and while awake.

55. He would not beseech for any position other than serving (Lord) Śrī Kṛṣṇa. After having gained firm devotion at his lotus feet one becomes full without any break.

56-58a. A person holding always firm faith and devotion to that adorable and content Brahman would elevate a crore of his ancestors and a hundred of his maternal grandfather. After having elevated sportively a hundred (of the ancestors) of his father-in-law, (he would elevate) a hundred of his male and female servants, mother and wife, a devotee of (Lord) Kṛṣṇa would certainly go to the world of cows.

58b-59a. A person entertaining desire would have birth, sufferings due to God of Death and be a householder desirous of pleasures, as long as he does not serve (Lord) Kṛṣṇa.

59b-60. In whose ear the mystic formula of (Lord) Viṣṇu enters from the mouth of the preceptor, that moment itself the God of Death erases the writing (on the forehead) out of fear. (Lord) Brahmā places the *madhuparka*[1] etc., in front of him.

61. (Such a person) would pass this way after crossing the world of mine. There is no return for him even after a crore of hundreds of *kalpas*.

62. Dreadful sins committed in crores of births would desert and run away from him just as the serpents (do) (at the sight of) Vainateya to (son of Vinatā) (Garuḍa).

63. (Lord) Kṛṣṇa would always cut asunder his past deeds, both meritorious and sinful, with His sharp-edged disc.

64. Death and decrepitude desert him fearing the disc. Otherwise, the *sudarśana* (disc of Kṛṣṇa) would cut them into hundred pieces.

65. There is no doubt that one goes to the Goloka after discarding the mortal coil. After reaching there he takes a divine body and always serves Lord Śrī Kṛṣṇa.

66. The devotee would stay in the Goloka as long as (Lord) Kṛṣṇa stays there. A devotee would regard the transient age of (Lord) Brahmā as a minute.

CHAPTER FIFTEEN

The Dialogue between Mālāvat and Kālapuruṣa

The Brahmin said :

1. O pious lady ! (Tell me) of what disease your husband has died now. I am a physician and I know the treatment for all the diseases.

2. I can resuscitate sportively, by means of great wisdom, a person almost dead or dead seven days back on account of a disease.

3. I am capable of bringing the Lord of Death, Yama, Kāla (time) and Disease in front of you bound just as a hunter would bind an animal.

4. O beautiful one ! I know the cause of the diseases and the means of arresting the spread of the diseases in the bodies of the mortals.

5. I know the ways of removing the deranged and inauspicious seed of a disease according to the medical lore.

6. I know the way of resuscitating a person discarding his life by means of *yoga* or due to grief, by the principles of *yoga*.

7. After listening to the words of the brahmin, the pure and chaste Mālāvatī smiled and replied him with affection.

Mālāvatī said:

8. Wonderful ! What extraordinary words I have heard from the mouth of a boy ? He is seen to be a very young child by his age. But his wisdom excels those of the well-versed in *yoga*.

9. You have resolved to revive my dead husband. The words of the pious do not go wrong. My husband would be revived this very moment.

10. The foremost among the knowers of the scriptures would resuscitate my husband afterwards. You are fit to tell me whatever I ask you on account of doubt.

11. I am not capable of asking you in the assembly in the presence of my impetuous husband after his resuscitation.

12. Brahmā and the other gods present in the assembly and yourself, the foremost among the learned in the scriptures, none of you is my lord.

13. No one is to be censured if the husband does not protect his wife. If he does not govern, there would be no protector in the world.

14. In the same way, the gods, Indra, Brahmā, Rudra and others do not have the ability (to protect). You should understand the relationship between the wife and husband. The husband is the lord of his wife.

15. The husband is her lord, leader, governor, nourisher and protector. There is no favourite deity, or a respectable one or a preceptor excelling the husband.

16. A girl born in a good family remains subservient to her spouse. An independent one is certainly wicked and crooked by nature.

17. The wicked one would serve other men. That vile lady born of a bad family would always censure her husband.

18. I am the daughter of Citraratha and the wife of Upabarhaṇa. O brahmin ! I am the daughter-in-law of the King of *gandharvas* and always devoted to my husband.

19. O Foremost among those learned in the scriptures ? You are capable of accomplishing everything. You bring Kāla (time), Yama and the daughter of Mṛtyu to my presence.

20. After listening to the words of Mālāvatī, the brahmin, foremost among those learned in the scriptures, called all of them to the assembly and made them visible to her.

21-22. The pious Mālātī beheld the daughter of Mṛtyu at first. She had a dark complexion. She had a dreadful form. She was wearing red garments. She was smiling, calm, compassionate and very chaste. She had six arms. She was on the left side of her lord Kāla accompanied by her sixty-four daughters.

23-26. That chaste lady then beheld Kāla, a part of (Lord) Nārāyaṇa in front of her. He had a dreadful form and hideous appearance. He had the lustre of the sun of summer. He had six faces, sixteen arms, twentyfour eyes and six legs. He had a dark complexion. He was wearing a red garment. He was lord of the lord. He had a form that would destroy all. He was the presiding lord of time. He was the lord of all beings. He was venerable and eternal. He had slightly smiling and cheerful face. He had an excellent string of rosary leads and was repeating (the name) of (Lord) Kṛṣṇa, the Supreme Brahman and lord of his own self.

27. That chaste lady then beheld the inconquerable host of diseases. They were very old. Yet they were sucking the breast of their mothers.

28-29. She then beheld Yama, the son of Ravi (Sun) in her front. He had stout leg and black complexion. He was a virtuous person. He was repeating (the name of) the Supreme Brahman, the venerable and eternal one. He was a judge of virtues and bad deeds. He was the embodiment of virtue. He governed the sinners also.

30. On beholding them, Mālāvatī, the most pious woman, having a cheerful face and look, first asked Yama.

Mālāvatī said :

31. O Dharmarāja ! One deep-rooted in virtue! One proficient in Dharmaśāstra! O Lord ! Why did you take away my husband violating the time ?

Yama said :

32. No one in the world dies unless the time has come. O pious woman ! I do not take away anyone without the will of God.

33. Myself, Kāla, the daughter of Mṛtyu and the invincible diseases take away by the will of God by the trickling of time.

34. Whomsoever the discerning daughter of Mṛtyu approaches by the trickling of time, I take away that person. You ask her the reason for that.

Mālāvatī said :

35. O Daughter of Mṛtyu ! You are also a woman. You know the grief due to (the death of) the husband. Why have you taken away my husband while myself, his sweet heart, is living ?

The daughter of Mṛtyu said :

36. I have been created by Brahmā for this task in the past. It is not possible for me to abandon (this task) even after a long penance.

37-38. O Beautiful lady ! If a splendrous chaste woman, among all chaste women, is capable of reducing me to ashes in this existence, all my miseries would end them. (I would not mind) what befalls and would befall to my sons and husband.

39. Myself and my sons, the diseases, have been impelled by Time. You know it from me certainly neither myself nor my sons are at fault.

40. You ask the great *kāla*(Time), the knower of virtue, in this assembly of the virtuous. O Pious lady ! You may then do what is appropriate.

Mālāvatī said :

41. O *kāla* (Time)! Witness of the actions ! Embodiment of action ! Eternal one ! A part-manifestation of (Lord) Nārāyaṇa ! Venerable one! Obeisance to you, the Supreme one.

42. O Lord ! How have you taken away my husband, when I am alive ? O Mine of compassion! You are omniscient. You know the grief of all the people.

Kālapuruṣa said :

43. (O Chaste lady !) Who am I ? Who is Yama? Who is the daughter of Mṛtyu ? Who are the diseases ? We always wander upholding the directions of the Lord.

44. Primordial Nature, (Lords) Brahmā, Viṣṇu, Śiva and others, the gods, the foremost sages, Manus, the mortal and all the beings are all his creations.

45. The learned yogins contemplate his lotus feet. They always mutter the meritorious names of that Supreme soul.

46. The wind blows and the Sun shines being afraid of him. Being commanded by him, (Lord) Brahmā is the creator and Viṣṇu is the protector.

47. Under his direction, (Lord) Śaṅkara is the destroyer of the entire world. Under his direction, the Lord of Virtue is the witness of the actions (of people).

48. The circle of zodiacal signs wander at his command. The guardian deities of the quarters and their regents are the upholders of his directive.

49. The trees bear flowers and fruits at his command. O Pious Mālāvatī ! They bear and yield at the appropriate time.

50. The earth having forbearance, supports all beings and holds water at his command. (The earth) does not tremble out of fear.

51. Illusion is always stupefied all of a sudden by his illusion. *Prakṛti*, the mother of all the beings, is afraid of him.

52. The scriptures, which have an insight into the objects do not have an comprehension of that Lord. All the *purāṇas* glorify him.

53. (Lords) Brahmā and Viṣṇu serve him. The great Virāṭ is only a sixteenth part of the Blessed one. It is the splendour of the Lord.

54. He is the Lord of all, the person governing Time, and Death of Death. He is the most Supreme. You meditate the (Lord) Kṛṣṇa for the destruction of all impediments.

55. That Mine of compassion would confer all your desires (and restore your) husband. The person who has sent all of us here is the conferer of all prosperity.

56. O Śaunaka ! After having stated thus, the Kālapuruṣa kept quiet. The brahmin resumed to tell his story again.

CHAPTER SIXTEEN

The Conversation between Viṣṇu and Mālatī on Medical Treatment

The brahmin said :

1. O Auspicious maiden ! You have beheld *kāla* (Time), Yama, the daughter of Mṛtyu and the hosts of diseases. What is your doubt now ? You may ask me now.

2. After listening to the words of the brahmin the pious Mālāvatī got pleased. She then asked the lord of the world the question that she had in her mind.

Mālāvatī said:

3. You have stated that disease takes away the lives of beings. It's different causes have been explained in the scriptures.

4. You are fit to explain me in detail the means of preventing the onslaught of unavoidable and inauspicious disease.

5. You tell me everything that is good whether asked by me or not, whether known to me or not. You are the preceptor. You are affectionate towards the indigent.

6. After hearing the words of Mālāvatī, (Lord) Janārdana (Viṣṇu) in the guise of a brahmin began to explain the medical science and its principle.

The brahmin said :

7. I salute Lord Kṛṣṇa, the knower of all principles, the cause of all causes, and the seed of the root cause of the scriptures and the ancillary texts.

8. That lord of the form of the root cause of all auspiciousness and eternal one created the four *vedas*, the above of auspiciousness.

9. Beholding the *vedas*–Ṛgveda, Yajurveda, Sāmaveda and Atharvaveda, Lord Brahmā reflected on their sense and made the medical science.

10-11. After creating the fifth *veda*, the Lord gave it to Bhāskara (Sun). The Sun-god made an independent treatise from that. The Sun-god then imparted his disciples the medical text made by him. They then created further medical treatises.

12. O Pious one ! You listen to me for the names of those learned men and the treatises made by them which are the root-cause of the destruction of disease.

13-14. Dhanvantari, Divodāsa, Kāśīrāja, Aśvinīkumāras, Nakula, Sahadeva, Arki (Yamarāja), Cyavana, Janaka, Budha, Jābāla, Jājali, Paila, Karatha and Agastya — these are the sixteen experts in the scriptures and allied texts and destroyers of diseases.

15 O Chaste lady ! The venerable Dhanvantari composed the outstanding treatise Cikitsātattvavijñāna at first.

16. Divodāsa composed the work called *cikitsādarpana*. Kāśirāja made the excellent (work) *cikitsākaumudī*.

17. The Aśvinikumāras composed thc *cikitsāsāratantra* and Bhramaghna. Nakula composed the treatise *vaidyakasarvasvatantra*.

18. Sahadeva composed the Vyādhisindhuvimardana. Yamarāja made the great *jñānārṇavatantra*.

19. The venerable sage Cyavana composed the *jīvadāna*. The ascetic Janaka composed the *vaidyasandehabhañjana*.

20. The son of Moon (Mercury) (Budha), (made) the *śarvasāra* and Jābāla, the *tantrasāraka*. The sage Jājali composed the *vedāṅgasāratantra*.

21. Paila (composed) the *nidāna* and Karatha, the foremost treatise *sarvadhara*. Kumbhasambhava (Agastya) composed the treatise *dvaidhanirṇava*.

22. These are the sixteen basic treatises on medical treatment capable of rooting out diseases and bringing strength.

23. After having churned the milky ocean of Āyurveda with the mystic formula of wisdom, the learned have extracted the butter.

24. O Beautiful lady ! After having read these treatises in order and the divine *bhāskarasaṁhitā*, I have known the Āyurveda, basis of all things.

25. The ability of a physician lies in the knowledge about the nature of the disease and the suppression of pain. A physician is not the master of one's longevity.

26. One is said to be a physician if he knows Āyurveda, has true knowledge of treatment and is virtuous and compassionate.

27. The most cruel fever is the father of all diseases and unavoidable. (The fever personified is) a devotee of (Lord) Śiva, an ascetic, very cruel and deformed.

28. (He is) dreadful, three-footed and three-headed. (He has) six arms and nine eyes. Ashes (are his) weapons. (He) is fierce. (He) resembles Yama (god of death), the *kālāntaka* (one that puts an end to the life).

29. Indigestion is its progenitor. Biles, phlegm and wind are the three causes of indigestion. They give pain to the living beings.

30. Fevers are of three kinds arising from wind, arising from biles and produced by phlegm. The fourth kind is that produced by (the combination of) these three defects.

31-33. Sixty-four diseases are known to be from the modifications of the white leprosy, jaundice, leprosy, tumour, the enlargement of spleen, colic, fever, dysentery, diarrhoea, consumption, ulcer, a kind of jaundice, stranguary, enlargement of spleen, derangement of blood, chronic urinary disease, *kabja*, goda,[1] goitre, vertigo, fever arising frrom the three deranged tumours and cholera of severe type.

34. These are the sons of the daughter of Mṛtyu and decrepitude is her daughter. Decrepitude always roams the earth in the company of her brothers.

35. These do not approach a disciplined person possessing the knowledge of the means (of protecting himself). They flee away on seeing him just like the serpents (do on seeing) the Vainateya (Garuḍa).

36. (Washing) the eyes with water, exercise, rubbing the soles with oil, applying oil in the ears and on the head keeps at bay old age and disease.

37. Walking in the spring, warming oneself moderately in front of the fire and enjoying the company of a young woman at the appropriate time would also arrest the advent of old age.

38. Bathing in the cold water of a pond, besmearing sandal paste and enjoying breeze would also arrest the advent of decrepitude.

39. Old age would not approach a person bathing in hot water in the rainy season, avoiding the use of hard water and eating balanced food at the appropriate time.

40. Decrepitude would not approach a person avoiding the consumption of pungent things in the autumn, avoiding roaming in that (season), bathing in the pond and eating even food.

41. Decrepitude would not approach a person bathing in the pond in the early winter, enjoying fire at the appropriate time and eating fresh and hot food.

42. Old age would not approach a person enjoying mild fire, eating fresh and hot food and bathing in hot water in the winter.

43. (One who) (eats) fresh meat and fresh food and enjoys (the company of) young woman, milky food and *ghee* would not become old.

44. One who partakes wholesome food when hungry, drinks water when thirsty and chews the betels daily would not become old.

45. Old age would not approach a disciplined person partaking curd, clarified butter, butter and molasses daily.

46. Accompanied by her brothers and with pleasure, decrepitude would go to a person partaking dry meat, enjoying (the company of) old woman, rising sun and fresh curd.

47. O Beautiful woman ! Accompanied by her brothers old age goes with delight to those consuming curd in the night, enjoying (the company of) harlots and menstruous woman.

48-49. One who partakes food from a menstruous woman, an unchaste woman, a woman devoid of her son or husband, a female messenger to a paramour, the wife of a person conducting a sacrifice for a low caste person, and one devoid of menses would incur (the sin of) killing a brahmin. That old age approaches such a person along with that sin.

50. There is always firm friendship for sins with diseases. Sin is the basis of disease and decrepitude. It is certainly the basis of obstacle.

51. Sin engenders disease, decrepitude, poverty, unhappiness and grief.

52. Hence on account of fright pious men in Bhārata do not commit sin that is a great enemy, basis of all defects and inauspicious.

53-54. Just as the serpents (would do at the sight of) Vainateya (Garuḍa), diseases run away beholding a person practising his code of conduct, an initiated one, a devotee of (Lord) Hari, a person devoted to his preceptor, gods and guests, one intent on practising penance, one practising austerities and fasting and one who always frequents the sacred places.

55. Old age do not approach such people. Hosts of diseases cannot conquer them. But it should be known that (the diseases) subdue everyone if the time is adverse.

56. O Pious woman ! It was told by me that the fever produces all diseases. (Vitiation of) biles, phlegm and wind are the three causes of fever.

57. O Pious lady ! Listen to me as to how these enter the human body and the different means for their removal.

58. In the absence of food when there is growing hunger, biles is produced in the (nerve centre) *maṇipūraka* in the living beings.

59. Drinking water immediately after eating the fruit of palmyra or bilva also produces biles capable of taking away one's life at once.

60. (Serving) hot water on the head and using sour things in the (month of) *bhādra* (August-September) and eating when one is under the spell of fate, biles is produced in him.

61-63. The coriander mixed with sugar and ground well with cold water, gram, all the products got from a cow except curd and butter milk, ripe fruits of palmyra and bilva, all items relating to sugarcane, ginger, soup of green gram, ground with sesamum and mixed with sugar are capable of destroying biles at once and are an excellent bestower of strength and nourishment. These are the remedies destroying biles. Now you learn from me other things.

64-67. Bathing after taking food, drinking water without thirst, (use of) sesamum oil, sticky oil and juice of myobabllan, stale food, butter milk, ripe banana fruit, curd, rain water, sugar mixed with water and using sticky water, coconut juice, bathing in dirty old water, ripe fruit of *taruguñjā*, ripe cucumber fruit, bathing in the pond in the rainy season and (eating) radish are the cause of phlegm. It has its origin in the (nerve-centre) *brahmarandhra* causing the destruction of one's great strength.

68-71. O *gandharva* lady! Perspiration due to fire, (use of) parched things, besmearing with refined (baked) oil, wandering, eating dry things, partaking dry and ripe yellow myrobalan, unripe *piṇḍāraka*, unripe banana fruit, *vesavāra*,[1] *sindhuvāra*,[2] abstaining from food and drink *rocanā* (a kind of yellow pigment) powder together with *ghee*, dry sugar together with ghee, pepper, fig, dry ginger, jīvaka and honey these ingredients remove the phlegm at once and give strength and nourishment. You now listen to the root cause of wind.

72-74. Walking, running and cutting soon after taking good, heat of fire, wandering and having intercourse frequently, having the union with an old woman, mental tormentation, (consuming) extremely dry (food), abstaining from food, fight, quarrel, harsh words, fear and grief are the only causes of wind. It has its origin in the nerve-centre of *ājñā*. Listen to me for its remedy.

75-79. Ripe banana fruit, water mixed with sugar together with seeds, coconut juice, fresh butter milk, cake made of flour, sweet curd from the buffalo, fresh food, stale food, jujube fruit, cold water, particular variety of refined oil, sesamum oil, coconut, palmyra, date, hot myrobalan juice, bathing in cold or hot water, cooling sandal water, cooling bed made of lotus leaf and cooling fans— I have told you these O Child ! as destroying wind at once. There are three kinds of wind for men— caused by pain, produced by torment and born of desire.

80. I have described you the hosts of diseases and the different treatises composed by saints for the destruction of diseases.

81. All these treatises are capable of destroying diseases. Very rare means and elixirs of life (have been described) in them.

82. O Pious lady ! It is not possible to describe even in the course of one year the full sense of all these treatises composed by the learned.

83. O Good lady ! Tell me of what diseases your husband has died. O Pious lady! I will devise the means for his revival, Sauti said.

84. After hearing the words of the brahmin, the *gandharva* daughter of Citraratha began narrating her story with delight.

Mālāvatī said :

85-86. My husband out of shame in the assembly discarded his life by ascetic practices on account of the curse of (Lord) Brahmā. O Brahmin ! You listen to me for the interesting rare and auspicious narrative. Unless a person comes to grief, it is impossible for attaining the good.

87. O learned one ! You restore my dear husband to me. I will salute you and go back to my house with my lord.

88. On hearing the words of Mālāvatī, (Lord) Janārdana in the form of a brahmin hastened to the assembly of gods leaving that place.

CHAPTER SEVENTEEN

The Dialogue between Lord Viṣṇu and the Gods and the Greatness of Lord Viṣṇu

Sauti said :

1. Beholding the brahmin, the assembly of gods rose up from their seats and welcomed him. Then there was a mutual conversation in that assembly.

2. The gods did not know that it was Lord Hari (Viṣṇu) in the guise of a brahmin. They had forgotten the order of events on account of the spell of (Lord) Viṣṇu.

3. O Brahmin ! The brahmin addressed the gods and spoke sweet words of truth and benevolence for the living beings.

The brahmin said :

4. This daughter of Citraratha and the wife of Upabarhaṇa being tormented by grief requested for the revival of her husband.

5. O Gods ! Tell me what is appropriate for being done in this regard now.

6. The pious, illustrious and outstanding lady is intent on cursing all the gods. After having spoken (conciliatory words) to that pious lady for the sake of your welfare, I have come to you.

7. You have eulogised (Lord) Hari at the Śvetadvīpa. Why your Lord Viṣṇu has not yet come to you here ?

8. There was a voice from the sky that Lord Keśava (Viṣṇu) would come later. How has that irrevocable statement in the air become false ?

9. After hearing the words of the brahmin (Lord) Brahmā, the preceptor of the world, himself, spoke true. beneficial and extremely auspicious words.

Brahmā said :

10. My son Nārada being cursed to become a *gandharva* Upabarhaṇa again discarded his life by ascetic practices on account of my curse.

11. He has to stay on the earth for a period of a lakh *yugas.* After being born as a *śūdra* he would again become my son.

12. O Foremost brahmin ! A little period of his life remains. He has (a balance) of a thousand years of his life now.

13. By the grace of (Lord) Viṣṇu I would myself revive him in such a way that certainly no curse would affect him in the future.

14. O Brahmin ! You have told me that (Lord) Hari has not come here. (Lord) Hari is omnipresent and the soul of everything. How can there be an embodied form for his own self ?

15. He is the Supreme Brahman, an embodiment of free will. He is an embodiment conferring His grace on His devotees. The omniscient one beholds all the things. He is omnipresent and eternal.

16. 'Viṣ' is an expression of pervasiveness and 'nu' an expression (meaning) everywhere. He is omnipresent and universal soul and hence he is glorified as Viṣṇu.

17. Whether one is pure or impure or has attained any state, if he remembers the 'lotus eyed' (Lord Viṣṇu), he becomes pure internally and externally.

18. O Brahmin ! Whoever remembers (Lord) Viṣṇu at the commencement or in the middle or at the end of an act as per the *vedas,* his act becomes completed.

19. I am the creator, (Lord) Hara is the destroyer and Dharma is the witness of all acts upholding His command.

20. Kāla destroys the world and Yama governs the sinners. By his command Mṛtyu approaches all always on account of fear.

21. *Prakṛti* (nature), who governs all, who is the first being and the mother of all (beings) in the past, carries out His comment with fright in front of him.

Maheśvara said :

22. From which family of the sons of Brahmā you had your birth ? After studying the *vedas* have you learnt their essence ?

23. O Brahmin ! You are the disciple of a sage of what name? Although you are a child you now possess (a splendour) excelling that of the Sun.

24. You are making a mockery of the gods and (Lord) Viṣṇu, our master. Do you know not the Supreme Soul, the master dwelling in the heart ?

25. When that Supreme one has gone, all the physical frame of the beings fall down. All beings go behind him as the retinue would follow a monarch.

26-27. The individual soul, the mind, knowledge, consciousness, the life breath, organs, intellect, retentive power, firmness, remembrance, sleep, compassion, lassitude, hunger, thirst, nourishment, faith, satisfaction, desire, forbearance, and bashfulness are all known to be His reflections.

28. When the Lord is intent on going away, His energy goes in front of Him. All these (above mentioned)and the energy uphold His command.

29. When the Lord stays on, an embodied person is proficient in doing all acts. When he has departed, one becomes an untouchable, a corpse to be discarded. Which person would not recognise Him ?

30. (Lord)Brahmā, the creator of the world and an agent of all acts, incapable of perceiving Him, meditates at the lotus feet (of the Lord) incessantly.

31. (Lord) Brahmā performed a penance for a lakh yugas (directed towards) Śrīkṛṣṇa. Then he became wise and capable of creating the world.

32. I have performed penance towards (Lord) Hari for a long innumerable period. My mind did not get satisfied. Who would get satisfied in good things (One would desire more).

33. Now I wander everywhere indifferent to all actions singing the glory of His name with five faces.

34. By the virtue of singing the glory of His name death goes away from me. Death runs away from me beholding me repeating His name always.

35. I am the destroyer of all the Universal egg (namely the created Universe). I am known as the conquerer of death by the virtue of singing the glory of His name and penance for a period (directed towards Him).

36. (After the elapse of) the period I get dissolved in that. I become manifest again. By His grace Time cannot destroy me and there is no death for me.

37. The person who is at Goloka, is at Vaikuṇṭha as well as at Śvetadvīpa. O Brahmin ! There is no difference between the part manifestation and the person having part manifestations just like the fire and the spark.

38-39. The *manvantara* period consists of seventy-one divine *yugas.* When the twenty-eighth Indra is gone, the day of Brahmā, of the hundred years of life of Brahmā, qualified by this reckoning (comes to an end) at the fall of the winking of the eye of the Supreme Being, (Lord) Viṣṇu.

40. I am the foremost among the digits of the Supreme Soul (Lord) Kṛṣṇa. I do not know anyone who can fathom, the greatness of that being.

41. O Śaunaka ! After having stated thus (Lord) Śaṅkara (Śiva) stopped talking. Dharma, the witness of all actions began to speak.

Dharma said:

42-43. How could there by such delusion for sages like you to state that (Lord) Viṣṇu, whose hands and feet reach everywhere, whose eye beholds everything and who is the soul of all the beings and who is visible and invisible for wicked people, has not yet come to the assembly.

44. Where there is censure of great men, good people would not listen to it. The despiser would certainly go to (the hell) *kumbhīpāka* along with the listeners.

45. After having listened to the censure of great people by the gods, a wise man would get free from all sins and would acquire merits difficult to get by remembering Śrī Viṣṇu.

46-47. One who despises (Lord) Viṣṇu knowingly or unknowingly, one who listens (to such slander) or the vile person who laughs in the assembly (after hearing such despise) would be tormented in the (hell) *kumbhīpāka* for a period of the life of Brahmā. O Brahmin ! That place would become impure just like the cup of wine.

48. Even the animal that hears that would certainly go to hell. In the past (Lord) Brahmā has specified three kinds of censure of (Lord) Viṣṇu.

49. A wretched foolish person (slanders) Him that He is imperceptible and hence does not recognise Him, or that He is equal to other gods.

50. There is no redemption for such a person for hundred years of (Lord) Brahmā. A person who slanders the preceptor or the father, gets entangled in the *kālasūtra* (a particular kind of hell) as long as the moon and sun last.

51. (Lord) Viṣṇu is the preceptor, progenitor of all beings, bestower of wisdom, nourisher, protector, rescuer from fear and conferrer of boon in the three worlds.

52. O Foremost among brahmins ! After hearing the words of these three, (he) smiled and again spoke to those gods sweet words.

The Brahmin said:

53-54. O Virtuous ones ! Eh ! What slander have I made of (Lord) Viṣṇu ? I had told that (Lord) Hari had not come and statement in the sky has become vain. O Gods ! Speak the truth for the sake of *dharma* (righteousness). If anyone is partial in an assembly, he would convey a hundred (of his ancestors to hell).

55. You are all blessed. You say that (Lord) Viṣṇu is always omnipresent. If it is so why you all had been to the Śvetadvīpa for the sake of (gaining) a favour.

56. If there is certainly no difference between the partmanifestation, the whole and the soul, why you all worship the whole being ignoring the digit (partmanifestation).

57. Though (Lord) Kṛṣṇa is difficult to be adored even after a crore of births and impossible to be attained by the wicked, there is strong desire for men to worship Him.

58. The mean as well as the great desire (to attain) the supreme position. They desire to get the moon, just like a dwarf would do with his hands.

59-60. Just as (Lord) Viṣṇu is a resident of the Śvetadvīpa, and there are the matter, you gods Brahmā, Īśa, Dharma, the guardians of the quarters and the presiding deities in this world, there are (gods) Brahmā, Viṣṇu, Śiva and others, the gods, animate and inanimate beings in (other worlds in) the universe. How many such are there in every universe?

61. Who is capable of counting the universes and gods ? (Lord) Kṛṣṇa, the embodiment of blessing the devotees is the master of all.

62. The cherished Vaikuṇṭha is above all the Brahmāṇḍa. The Goloka extending to fifty crores of *yojanas* is above that.

63. The consort of (goddess) Lakṣmī (Lord Viṣṇu) having four arms is eternal in Vaikuṇṭha surrounded by his courtiers such as Sunanda, Nanda, Kumuda and others.

64. The consort of Rādha, (Lord) Kṛṣṇa having two hands, is eternal in the Goloka, in the company of the cowherdesses and others and the deputy courtiers having two hands.

65. He is the complete and perfect brahman, the soul of all beings and the embodiment of sweet will. He always indulges in amorous sports (*rāsa*) in the Vṛndāvana (bower of holy basil).

66. The ascetics and pious meditate always that blemishless and circular light effulgent like a crore of suns.

67-68. The pious devotees of (Lord) Viṣṇu meditate that dark (form resembling the) fresh (rain bearing) cloud endowed with two hands, wearing yellow dress, enchanting like crores of gods of love, abode of divine sport, captivating, having youthful eyes, ever tranquil and smiling and serve that embodiment of truth.

69. O *vaiṣṇavas* ! You ask me again and again as to whose descendant I am and the disciple of which foremost sage.

70. O *assembly* of gods ! You know that these words of wisdom (are) from him in whose line I am born and this boy is a disciple.

71. O Lord of the gods ! O Lord of the celestials! You revive that *gandharva* quickly. (You know) which fool (has indulged) in worthless inquiry. What use (in indulging) in verbal debate ?

72. O Śaunaka ! After having spoken thus, (Lord) Janārdana in the guise of a brahmin boy, ceased talking and smiled.

CHAPTER EIGHTEEN

The Revival of the *Gandharva* and Mālatī's Eulogy of the Supreme God

Sauti said:

1. Then the gods led by (Lords) Brahmā and Īśāna being deluded by the spell of (Lord) Viṣṇu went with the brahmin to Mālatī.

2. (Lord) Brahmā sprinkled water out of the *kamaṇḍalu* (wooden water pot) over the corpse. (Then that *gandharva*) gained the functions of the mind and a handsome body.

3. (Lord) Śiva himself, the bliss of wisdom, conferred on him the gift of wisdom. (Lord) Dharma himself (bestowed on him) virtue. The brahmin gave him life.

4. The digestive fire was revived by the mere sight of the Fire-god. By the mere sight of the god of love all the desires got firm.

5. By the power of the Wind-god, the natural form of the life-breath of the world, the life-breath and exhalation were revived.

6-7. By the mere power of the sun, the power of sight was restored. Being beheld by (goddess) Sarasvatī, speech (came to him). By the sight of (goddess) of Fortune, grace (was restored). The corpse did not get up even then. It was lying as an inanimate thing. But not being presided over by the soul, he did not get the consciousness.

8. On the words of (Lord) Brahmā, the pious lady glorified the Supreme god after bathing quickly in the river and wearing the washed clothes.

Mālāvatī said :

9-17. I salute that Supreme Soul, the cause of all causes, without whom all the beings in the world are corpses, who does not get stained (by everything), who is of the form of a witness of all the actions of all the people, who is not preceived by all, although he is always omnipresent, who is the creator of the *prakṛti,* the most supreme possessing the three qualities and the progenitor of (Lords) Brahmā, Viṣṇu, Śiva and others, by serving whom (Lord) Brahmā is permanently the creator of the world, (Lord) Viṣṇu is the protector and (Lord) Śaṅkara is the destroyer, whom all the gods, sages, Manus, *siddhas* (accomplished souls), ascetics and pious men meditate, (who is) always above the *prakṛti* (Nature), (who is) endowed with a form and formless, an embodiment of sweet will, master, outstanding, worthy of adoration, bestower of boon, worthy of praise, cause of favours, fruit of penance, seed of penance, confererrof the fruits of penance, himself of the form of penance, a form of all things everywhere, the basis of all, the seed of all, action, the fruit of actions, the conferrer of their fruits, their seed, the cause of their destruction, himself of the form of lustre, and an embodiment of favouring the devotees.

It is not possible for his devotees to serve him or meditate him without an idol.

18-31. I am a destitute incapable of extolling that spherical lustre equal to that of a crore Suns, a very attractive form that is captivating, dark like the fresh cloud, having eyes like the lotus of the autumn, possessing a face as the full moon of the autumn endowed with a gentle smile, having the beauty of a crores of God of love, is an abode of sport, is an attractive one, is besmeared with sandal paste all over the body, is adorned with gem-studded ornaments,– is having two hands, is holding the flute in his hand, is wearing yellow silk dress, is young in age, is tranquil, consort of Rādhā, is an endless one, is surrounded by the cowherdesses in the solitude of a forest, is sometimes figuring as the central figure in the dance circle, is being attended by Rādhā, is sometimes wearing the dress of a cowherd and surrounded by the cowherd boys in the charming Vṛndāvana (bower of the holy basil) made lovely by the Śataśṛṅga hills, is guarding as a boy a herd of cows, is playing sweetly on the lute in the Pārijāta grove at Goloka on the banks of (river) Virajā that is the cause of enticing the cowherdesses, has four arms gracing somewhere in the disease-free Vaikuṇṭha, is the consort of (Goddess) Lakṣmī, is served by an assembly of courtiers having four arms, is making a part manifestation somewhere for the protection of the world, (is shining) in the form of Viṣṇu and served by Padmā (Goddess Lakṣmī) at Śvetadvipa,-(is shining) in the form of (Lord) Brahmā somewhere in the Brahmāṇḍa with a digit of his part manifestation, is a form of (Lord) Śiva, is a conferrer of good, is a form of Śiva as a part manifestation, is the support of all by means of his sixteenth part, is most supreme, is himself the Mahat and *Virāṭ* (the first progeny of Brahman), is having the entire universe in the pores of his skin, is making different manifestations sportively with a digit of his part manifestation for the protection of the world, is the eternal seed of those and dwells somewhere in the hearts of the ascetics, is of the form of life in the living beings, is the Supreme Soul, and is the master.

32. He is invisible. He is free from desire. He is the essence beyond the speech and mind. (Serpent) Ananta is incapable of extolling him with his thousand mouths.

33. The (Lords) Śiva, Brahmā, Gaṇeśa and Kārttikeya are incapable of extolling him. Illusion being stupefied by his illusion is not capable of extolling him.

34. (Goddess) Lakṣmī also cannot eulogise him. (Goddess) Sarasvatī becomes inert (and unable to glorify). The *vedas* are incapable of extolling. What to speak of a learned person, well-versed in the *vedas* ?

35. How shall I, a woman tormented by grief, extol that most supreme desireless person? After having spoken thus, that *gandharva* lady stopped (talking) and wept.

36-37a. Being afflicted by fear, she saluted the mine of compassion again and again. In the meanwhile (Lord) Kṛṣṇa, the Supreme soul and formless one accompanied by his powers presided over the body of her husband.

37b-38. (Her husband) got up quickly, held his lute after bathing and wearing the dress and made his obeisance to the assembly of gods and the brahmin standing in front of him. The drums sounded and the gods showered flowers (on them).

39. After beholding them, (the gods) conferred their blessings on them. The *gandharva* danced in front of the gods and sang for a while.

40. He got back his life by the favour of the gods. (Getting united) with his wife and parents, he became happy.

41-43. The *gandharva* Upabarnaṇa went back to the city of the *gandharvas* again. The chaste Mālāvatī gave away various gifts of innumerable gems and wealth to brahmins and fed them. She arranged for the recitation of the *vedas* and auspicious things. She arranged for different kinds of good festivals in the name of (Lord) Hari. The gods and (Lord) Hari in the form of a brahmin went back to their place.

44-46. O Śaunaka! I have described you everything including the excellent hymn. Whoever reads this meritorious hymn at the time of offering worship, that *vaiṣṇava* would get devotion and servitude to (Lord) Hari. A faithful person seeking a favour after reading (this hymn) with devotion and earnestness would certainly get the fruits of virtue, wealth, desire and beatitude. A seeker of learning gains learning and a person desiring for wealth gets the wealth.

47. A person wishing for a wife would get a spouse. A seeker of progeny would get progeny. A seeker of virtue would get virtue and a seeker of wealth would get fame.

48. A person banished from the kingdom would get his kingdom. A person deprived of his servants would get his servants. One afflicted by a disease would get free from the disease. A captive would become free from bondage.

49. A frightened one becomes free from fear. A person that has lost wealth would get the wealth. A person who has been seized by the *dasyus* (tribes) in a dense forest inhabited by wild beasts and tormented by forest fire would become free. A person drowned in an ocean (would be saved).

CHAPTER NINETEEN

Eulogy on (Lords) Viṣṇu and Śiva

Sauti said :

1. After having given away wealth to brahmins, Mālāvatī was delighted. For the sake of her husband she put on different kinds of dress.

2. She served him and offered him worship appropriate to the occasion. The connoisseur enjoyed his company with pleasure for a long time.

3-5. In privacy that disciplined lady made him remember the forgotten hymn, mode of worship and other formalities relating to (Lord) Hari imparted by (sage) Vasiṣṭha in days of yore. In privacy (the sage) Vasiṣṭha, the mine of compassion, taught the *gandharva* prince the hymn and amulet on (Lord) Śūlin (Śiva) that he had forgotten.

6. In this way the *gandharva* reigned in his hermitage, resembling the abode of Kubera, in the company of his kinsmen with great pleasure.

7. The other wives (of the *gandharva*) who had left him now and then, returned to him and they had regained their master with great delight.

Śaunaka said:

8-10. O Sauti ! It befits you to describe me the hymn, amulet, the procedure and formula for the worship of (Lord) Viṣṇu imparted specially to them in days of yore. You may also describe me the twelve syllabled formula and amulet etc. for (Lord) Śiva imparted by the sage Vasiṣṭha to the *gandharva* prince in the past. I have curiosity to listen to the hymn, amulet and formula relating to (Lord) Śaṅkara (Śiva) which destroys misfortune.

Sauti said :

11. You listen to the hymn, formula and amulet imparted (by the sage)and the hymn with which **Mālatī** extolled the Supreme lord.

12. Om ! Obeisance to the venerable lord of the dance circle. Oblation. This amulet of sixteen syllables, a wish-yielding tree, was given (by the sage).

13. (This amulet) of (Lord) Hari was imparted by (Lord) Brahmā to Kumāra (son of Śiva) at Puṣkara in the past. It was imparted by (Lord) Kṛṣṇa to (Lord) Śaṅkara (Śiva) at Goloka in the past.

14. The perennial meditation (process) of (Lord) Viṣṇu expounded in the *vedas* and very difficult to procure (was also imparted). All the offering and other formalities should be given (with the repetition) of this basic (formula).

15. I have listened to the extremely secret amulet from my father's mouth. O Brahmin ! It was given to my father by (Lord) Sūlin (Śiva) on the (banks of) the Ganges in the past.

16. That most wonderful (formula) was given by the consort of the cowherdesses (Lord Kṛṣṇa) to (the Lords) Śiva, Brahmā and Dharma in the dance-circle at Goloka graciously.

Brahmā said :

17-18. O the most fortunate consort of Rādhā ! O lord ! O kind one to the devotees ! Tell me, the (lord) Śiva and Dharma and the devotee the amulet known as 'the purifier of the universal egg' made explicit (by you earlier). Endowed with devotion I will impart it to my sons with your grace.

Śrī Kṛṣṇa said :

19. O Lords Brahmā, Īśa and Dharma ! I will impart you this supreme amulet. You have to guard this difficult one to be obtained.

20. As it is equal to my very life, it should not be imparted to all and sundry. This lustre that is enshrined in me is present in the amulet also.

21. Receiving this (amulet), O Brahmā ! You be the creator of the three worlds. O Śambhu! You become the destroyer and be equal to me in mundane existence.

22. O Dharma! Holding this (amulet), you become the witness of all acts. By my favour you be the conferrer of the fruits of penance.

23. (Lord) Hari himself is the sage, Gāyatrī the metre and myself, the lord of the world, the deity for this amulet (known as) *Brahmāṇḍapāvana* (the purifier of the universal egg).

24. The application of this amulet for the sake of virtue, wealth, desire and beatitude has been glorified. O Brahmā! The amulet gets accomplished by the repetition of it three lakhs times.

25. Whoever accomplishes mastery of the amulet, that person would become equal to me in lustre, gaining of perfection, wisdom and valour.

26. May *praṇava* (the syllable *om*) protect my head. May 'Obeisance to Rāmeśvara' guard my forehead. May 'Obeisance to Rādheśvara' (guard) my pair of eyes.

27. May (Lord) Kṛṣṇa protect my pair of ears. May 'O Hari' (guard) my nose. May the consort of Fire-god (protect) the tongue. May 'for Lord Kṛṣṇa' guard all around.

28. May the six syllables 'Oblations to Lord Kṛṣṇa' guard the throat. May '*hrīm* obeisance to Lord Kṛṣṇa' protect the face. May (the same words) preceded by *klīm* guard my two arms.

29. May the eight syllables 'Obeisance to the lord of the cowherdesses' protect the two shoulders. May (the words) 'Obeisance to the master of the cowherdesses' guard the rows of teeth and pair of lips.

30. May the sixteen syllabled formula 'Obeisance to the venerable Lord of dancing circle' itself guard the region of the chest.

31. May (the words) '*aim* oblations to (Lord) Kṛṣṇa' guard always my pair of ears. May (the words) '*om* oblations to (Lord) Viṣṇu' protect the cheek all around.

32. May (the words) '*om* obeisance to (Lord) Hari' guard always the back and feet. May (the words) '*om* oblations to the uplifter of the Govardhana (hill)' protect my entire body.

33. May Lord Kṛṣṇa guard me in the east. May Mādhava (consort of Lakṣmī) guard me in the south-east. May the lord of the cowherdesses protect me in the south. May the son of Nanda (cowherd chief) (guard) in the south-west.

34. May (Lord) Govinda (the grazer of cows) protect me in the west, and the lord of Rādhikā in the north-west. May the lord of dance guard in the north and (Lord) Acyuta himself on the north-east.

35. May the supreme (Lord) Nārāyaṇa guard me always all around. O Brahmā ! I have described you thus the most wonderful amulet.

36. (This amulet) equal to my life has been imparted to you. (Performance of) thousands of Aśvamedha and hundreds of Vājapeya sacrifices do not deserve (the merits) of a digit of wearing this amulet.

37-38. A wise man should wear this amulet after bathing and duly honouring the preceptor with dress, ornaments and sandal paste and making prostration. One would be liberated while living by the grace of this amulet. O Brahmin! One would become (Lord) Viṣṇu himself if he had accomplished (the mastery of) this amulet.

Sauti said:

39. O Śaunaka ! May you listen to the amulet and hymn on (Lord) Śiva and the formula imparted by (sage) Vasiṣṭha to the *gandharva.*

40. The formula, '*om* obeisance to the venerable (Lord) Śiva,' Oblation on the Lord was graciously imparted by sage Vasiṣṭha at Puṣkara in the past.

41. This formula was imparted by (Lord) Brahmā to Rāvaṇa (demon ruler of Laṅkā) in olden days. (Lord) Śiva himself imparted it to Bāṇa (a demon) and (sage) Durvāsa in days of yore.

42. All the best offerings etc., should be dedicated with this basic (formula). One should meditate (and do) one's daily practices such as meditation etc., expounded in the Vedas and accepted by all.

43. Om! Obeisance to (Lord) Mahādeva. Bāṇāsura said : O Maheśvara ! Most fortunate one ! O Master ! Kindly describe me the amulet called *saṁsārapāvana* (purifying the mundane existence) which you had expounded.

Maheśvara said :

44. O Child ! Listen to me. I will impart you the most wonderful amulet. I will impart you this one most difficult to get which has to be kept concealed.

45. In days of yore it was imparted to (sage) Durvāsa for the conquest of the three worlds.

46. O Venerable one ! The wise man who reverentially wears this amulet of mine would be able to conquer the three worlds sportively.

47. Prajāpati is the sage, Gāyatrī the metre and I, Maheśvara the presiding deity of this amulet (called) *saṁsārapāvana* (purifying the mundane existence). Its application in (matters relating to) virtue, wealth, desire and beatitude have been glorified.

48. The amulet gets accomplished by the repetition of it for five lakh times. One that has accomplished this amulet would become equal to me in lustre, acquisition of perfection and valour on earth.

49. May (Lord) Śambhu (Śiva) protect my head. May (Lord) Maheśvara protect my face, (Lord) Nīlakaṇṭha (blue throated) the row of teeth and (Lord) Hara himself the lower lip.

50. May (Lord) Candracūḍa (one wearing the crescent on the head) protect the throat, the Lord having the bull as the vehicle (protect) the shoulders, the blue-throated (Lord) (protect) the region of the chest and the Lord having the quarters as the dress, protect the back.

51. May the Lord of the universe guard all my limbs in all the directions always. May the (god remaining as a) column protect me always while I am asleep and awake.

52. O Bāṇa ! Thus I have imparted you the most wonderful amulet. It should not be imparted to all and sundry. It should be concealed with effort.

53. What benefit would accrue to a person by bathing in all the sacred waters, would certainly be obtained by wearing this amulet.

54. For a dull-witted person who would worship me without knowing this amulet, the formula repeated even a hundred lakh times would not be conferrer of benefits (for him).

Sauti said:

55. O Śaunaka ! I have described the amulet. Listen to the hymn (now). The excellent formula which is a wish-yielding tree was imparted by (sage) Vasiṣṭha in days of yore.

56-64. Om obeisance to (Lord) Śiva !

Bāṇāsura said:

I salute the best of gods, the master of the gods, the blue and tawny one, lord of the ascetics, seed of asceticism, the preceptor of the preceptor of ascetics, blissful, wisdom, the form of wisdom, seed of wisdom, the eternal one, the bestower of the fruits of penance, the conferrer of all prosperities, the form of penance, the seed of penance, the foremost wealth of the ascetics (whose wealth is penance), the foremost one, bestower of boons, adorable by the foremost accomplished persons and attendants (of Lord Śiva), the cause of enjoyment and emancipation, the person that enables us to cross the ocean of hell, spontaneously pleasing, having a cheerful face, an ocean of embodiment of compassion, possessing the lustre of snow, sandal paste, jasmine, moon and white water-lily, having the form of lustre of brahman, an embodiment of favouring the devotees, assuming manifold forms on account of different (conditions of) matter such as the forms of water, fire, sky, the suzerain lord, wind, moon, sun and the great master in order to confer sportively his own position on anybody, the lord that is the very life of the devotees and compassionate in favouring the devotees. How can I extol that lord, the undefinable master, beyond the (comprehension of) speech and mind, clad in tiger skin, seated on the bull, having the quarters as the dress, wielding the trident and the axe, smiling and having the crescent moon on his head, whom the *vedas* are incapable of eulogising ?

65-66. After having eulogised thus Bāṇa daily used to bow to (Lord) Śiva with reverence. The venerable sage Durvāsa also (repeated) this hymn imparted by (sage) Vasiṣṭha to the *gandharva* in the past. O Sage ! I have described you the great and most wonderful hymn on (Lord) Śiva.

67. Whoever reads this most meritorious hymn would certainly get the benefits of bathing in all the sacred waters.

68. One without progeny would get a son by listening to this hymn for one year with devotion after partaking *havis* (cooked food offered to the deity) and worshipping Lord Śiva.

69. A dipping leper and a person suffering severe colic would get rid of the disease by listening to this hymn for a month as per the statement of (sage) Vyāsa heard (by us).

70. A prisoner having no means of gaining release, would certainly become free by listening to this hymn for a month.

71. (A king) who had lost his kingdom would regain his kingdom by listening to the hymn for a month. A man who had lost his wealth would regain his wealth by listening to the hymn for a month with devotion.

72. A religious person seized by consumption would surely become free from the disease by listening to the hymn for a year by the grace of (Lord) Śiva.

73. O Brahmin ! Whoever listens this outstanding hymn with devotion, O Śaunaka ! There is nothing that could not be accomplished in the three worlds.

74. There can never be separation for him from the kinsmen on (the land of) Bhārata. There is no doubt that one would acquire imperishable great wealth.

75. Whoever reads (this hymn) with earnestness and great devotion for a month, such a person without a spouse would get a chaste, excellent and modest wife.

76. A very stupid and dull-witted person would obtain intellect and knowledge by listening (the hymn) for a month by the mere instruction of the preceptor.

77. One suffering from grief on account of his (past) deeds would certainly gain wealth by listening (the hymn) for a month by the grace of (Lord) Śiva.

78-79. (Such a person) would enjoy all the comforts in this world, gain fame and unattainable virtues of different kinds and reach the abode of (Lord) Śiva in the end. A person would become the foremost among the countries there and serve (Lord) Śiva by listening this excellent hymn daily in the three twilights.

CHAPTER TWENTY

The Narration of the Story of Upabarhana

Sauti said :

1-2. The *gandharva* Upabarhana spent merrily the remaining part of his life in the company of Mālāvatī and others in the uninhabited forest. The *gandharva* king rejoiced in the company of his sons and wives. He performed different kinds of excellent rites and acquired great merits.

3. The king enjoyed sovereignty in the mansion resembling that of Kubera (God of wealth and Yakṣas). He made merry with his ever youthful wife Suśīlā.

4. The *gandharva* king discarded his life along with his wife on the charming banks of the Ganges at the appropriate time and attained Vaikuṇṭha with pleasure.

5. Being a devotee of (Lord) Śiva he became an attendant on (Lord) Viṣṇu, the dark complexioned one endowed with four arms, at Vaikuṇṭha, by the grace of (Lord) Śiva and the service rendered by his son to (Lord) Viṣṇu.

6. The *gandharva* Upabarhaṇa performed the obsequies of his father. O Brahmin! He gave away wealth to the brahmins.

7. O Śaunaka ! He also discarded his life on account of the curse of (Lord) Brahmā. That wise man was born in the womb of a low caste woman from a brahmin.

8. The chaste Mālāvatī also performed the desired rites in the fire-pit at Puṣkara in Bhārata on the earth and discarded her life.

9. She was then born (as the daughter of) King Sṛñjaya, a descendant of Manu's race. That pious lady was meritorious and had memory of her past life.

10. That beautiful lady had craved for a boon (at the time of her death) that she should have Upabarhaṇa as her husband in the future also.

Śaunaka said :

11. You deserve to tell me how the *gandharva* Upabarhana was born from the womb of a *śūdra* woman from a *brahman.*

Sauti said :

12. There was a king named Drumila in the country of Kānyakubja. He had a chaste wife by name Kalāvatī, who was barren.

13. She became barren on account of the faults of her husband. By the command of her husband, she approached sage Nārada son of Kaśyapa, in a dreadful forest.

14. He was meditating Lord Kṛṣṇa and was glowing with the lustre of brahman. Having dressed herself well she stood in front of the sage awaiting the conclusion of his meditation.

15. She was neither able to go near nor stand even at a distance from him who was doing penance and was having the lustre of the midday Sun in the summer.

16-20. At the end of his meditation, the foremost sage deeply devoted to (Lord) Kṛṣṇa saw in front of him a very youthful beautiful lady, who had the complexion of charming *campaka* (flower), the eyes resembling the lotus of the autumn, the face resembling the full moon of the autumn, was adorned with gem (studded) ornaments, was afflicted by the weight of big buttocks, had stout hips and breasts, made beautiful by the yellow dress, was smiling and had red eyes, was captivated by the (attractive) form of the sage, was afflicted by the shafts of the god of love, exhibiting her breasts and loins desirous of having sexual union with him, was adorned by the mark of vermilion and ornaments, was shining with attractive collyrium, was endowed with the beauty of the red lac on the feet and resembled Urvaśī (nymph) in her form.

21. Beholding her the sage asked : Who are you in the uninhabited forest ? Whose wife are you ? How are you here? Tell me the truth, O Unchaste one !

22. After having heard the words of the sage, Kalāvatī trembled and spoke modestly remembering (Lord) Hari (Viṣṇu).

Kalāvatī said :

23. O Foremost brahmin ! I am a cowherdess and the wife of (King)Drumila. By the command of my husband I have come to you for the sake of progeny.

24. Impregnate me. You should not disregard a woman who had come voluntarily. Just like the all devouring fire, it will not be a stain on glorious people (like you).

25. The holy sage became angy on hearing the words of the low-caste woman. With his lips trembling with rage he spoke didactic and true words.

Kāśyapa said :

26. Whoever desires to give to others his mistress worthy of enjoyment, that lady would certainly desert that ignorant person states the *vedas.*

27. You will not again become worthy of being enjoyed by (King) Drumila. You have been rejected by a detached one. He will not accept you again.

28-29. A brahmin wanting in knowledge accepting a *śūdra* wife becomes truly a *caṇḍala.* He becomes unfit for the rites of the twice-borns (the first three castes), annual ceremonies of the parents, sacrificial rites, touching the stone (*śālagrāma* sacred for god Viṣṇu). The lotus-born (Brahmā) has stated so.

30. He himself goes to the (hell called) *Kumbhīpāka* after making fall his ancestors ten preceding and ten succeeding such as the maternal grandfathers and others.

31. The water of oblation (given by him to the manes) would only be urine and the ball of rice (would be) ordure. If he touches the *śālagrama* (he has) to fast for three nights.

32. His favourite deity will not accept the offering and water offered by him. The food (offered) by him will be like ordure for the ascetics and brahmins.

33. O Unchaste lady ! He will be tormented in the (hell) *kumbhīpāka* along with twenty one (generations of his kinsmen) till end. It is certain.

34. A vile brahmin who eats the remnants of food from the leaf of a *śūdra* would be deemed to be similar to him as declared by (sage) Aṅgira.

35. If a *śūdra* not having knowledge accepts a brahmin lady, he will be tormented in (the hell called) *kālasūtra* till the period of 14 Indras ends.

36. The brahmin lady would be tormented in the (hell) *kālasūtra* for a period having the duration of 18 Indras, being bitten by insects. It is certain.

37. After that the brahmin lady would take birth as a *caṇḍāla*. The *śūdra* would become a leper forsaken by his kinsmen.

38. O Śaunaka ! After having spoken thus the foremost sage stopped talking. The *śūdra* woman stood in front of him with her throat, lips and palate parched.

39. In the meanwhile (the nymph) Menakā was passing through that way. On seeing her loins and breasts the semen of the sage fell down.

40. The *śudra* woman who had bathed after the menses drank it that moment itself with delight. After saluting the sage she returned to her husband with delight.

41. After returning there the spouse saluted her handsome husband Drumila and narrated all the incidents that had caused the pregnancy.

42. After hearing the words of Kalāvatī, (Drumila) became delighted and spoke to his wife sweet and pleasing words.

Drumila said :

43. The semen virile of a great *vaiṣṇava* brahmin is in your womb. The child will be a *vaiṣṇava* and you will be a fortunate woman.

44. O chaste lady ! The woman from whose womb and the person from whose semen, a *vaiṣṇava* is born, hundreds of their ancestors attain Vaikuṇṭha (the abode of Lord Viṣṇu).

45. Those two also would go to Vaikuṇṭha city in the aerial vehicle set up with excellent gems that would terminate the birth, death and old age.

46. O Lady with auspicious face ! Go to the house of some brahmin. O Good lady ! You would then come to me in the city of (Lord) Hari.

47. After having spoken thus the cowherd king bathed, offered water oblation (to the manes), worshipped the favourite deity and gave away wealth to the brahmins.

48-54. He gave with pleasure four lakh horses, a lakh elephants, and hundred royal elephants in rut to the brahmins. Besides he gave five lakhs of Uccaiḥśravas (horses), a thousand chariots and three lakhs of carts to the brahmins with delight. Moreover he gave twelve lakhs of cows, three lakhs of buffaloes and three lakhs of royal swans to the brahmins happily. O Sage! He further gave merrily a lakh of pigeons, a hundred parrots and a lakh of male and female attendants to the brahmins. In addition he gave thousands of villages, hundreds of cities and hills of grains and rice to the brahmins with delight. He gave hundred crores of gold, thousand gems and a crore pots of gold coins to the brahmins with pleasure. He gave splendid vessels, innumerable ornaments and similar numbers of women adorned with gems to the brahmins with delight.

55. After giving away his kingdom, the great king remembered (Lord) Hari inwardly and outwardly. That cowherd then proceeded to Badari (a sanctified place known as Badarikāśrama, the hermitage of jujubes) hastily with delight.

56. After performing penance there for a month on the charming banks of the Ganges, he discarded his life by ascetic process in the presence of great sages.

57. He reached Vaikuṇṭha in the heavenly car of (Lord) Viṣṇu built with excellent gems in the company of the messengers of (Lord) Viṣṇu.

58. He attained the position of being an attendant of (Lord)Viṣṇu and hence became (known as) Haridāsa. O Śaunaka ! Now listen to the story of Kalāvatī.

59. After the death of her husband Kalāvatī wept aloud. She wanted to discard her life (by falling) in the fire. But she was protected (by the brahmin).

60. The brahmin addressed her 'O Mother' and in a moment escorted her with pleasure to his house enriched by gems.

61. That pious lady delivered an excellent child possessing the complexion of heated gold and glowing with the lustre of brahman in the house of the brahmin.

62-65. All the women in that place looked at that auspicious child conquering the midday sun of the summer with his lustre of brahman, excelling the god of love in his (handsome) form, having the face more auspicious than the moon, having the face resembling the autumnal moon, having the eyes resembling the autumnal lotus, possessing graceful hands and feet, having an attractive cheek, having the lotus feet bearing the marks of lotus and disc incomparable and lustrous, the pair of hands being incomparable and crying for breast(milk). After seeing the child the women went back to their abodes with delight.

66. The brahmin was delighted and danced (merrily) in the company of his sons and wives. That child grew up just like the moon in the bright fortnight.

67. The brahmin nourished her and the child as his (own) daughter.

CHAPTER TWENTY-ONE

The Release of Nārada from the Curse

Sauti said :

1. In course of time the boy duly grew up into five year old (boy). He remembered his past birth. He was endowed with wisdom. He always remembered the formula (learnt in the) past.

2. He always sang the glory of the fame, name and quality of (Lord) Kṛṣṇa. He would weep a while accompanied by dancing with horripilation on his body.

3-4. He would listen to ballads relating to the (Lord) Kṛṣṇa. That child, would stand there where the legends of (Lord) Kṛṣṇa (were recounted) with his entire body besmeared with dust. He desired to make an offering of dust. He would make image (of Lord Kṛṣṇa) out of mud and worship (Lord) Hari with dust.

5. O Sage ! If the mother would call the boy for morning food, the boy would reply his mother, 'I am worshipping (Lord) Hari.'

Śaunaka said :

6. What was the name of this boy in the previous birth ? You are fit to tell me the names and their etymologies.

Sauti said :

7. As this boy was born when there was a balance of the drought season and as he offered water at the time of his birth, he was known as Nārada.

8. That boy imparted *nāra*, wisdom to the boys. He had the memory of the conditions of his past life. He was a greatly learned person. Hence he was known as Nārada.

9. O Sage ! That boy was born from the semen of a saint Nārada. He was known as Nārada by the favour of Nārada.

Śaunaka said :

10. I have known the name of the child and its etymology. But why did the saint have the auspicious name Nārada ?

Sauti said :

11. The sage Nara, the son of Dharma blessed the childless Kaśyapa with a son. Hence he was known as Nārada.

Śaunaka said :

12. O Sauti ! Now I have heard the etymology of the child. Why was the son of Brahmā, born in the womb of a *śūdra*, known as Nārada ?

Sauti said :

13. Many men came out from the throat of (Lord) Brahmā in a different kalpa. Because that throat gave out men it was known as Nārada.

14. Then the boy was born from Nārada, from the region of the throat. Then (Lord) Brahmā gave him the auspicious name Nārada.

15. Now you listen attentively to the story of the child. What special benefit is there in delaying (the narration of) the secret ?

16. The cowherd boy grew up every day in the house of the brahmin. The brahmins protected her along with her son as (he would do) his daughter.

17. In the meanwhile brahmins came to the house of the brahmin. They were children aged five years having great lustre[1].

18. They were concealed and they excelled the midday sun of the summer. O Brahmin ! That householder offered them *madhuparka*[2] and other things and saluted them.

19. The foremost sages ate the fruits, roots and other things given by the brahmin at the appropriate time. The child ate the remnants (of food).

20. The fourth among the sages was pleased and imparted him (the boy) the mystic formula of (Lord) Kṛṣṇa. He became an attendant of those sages at the command of his mother and the brahmin.

21. Once as the mother of the child was going on a pathway in the night, she was bitten by a serpent. She died that moment itself remembering (the name of) (Lord) Hari.

22. That chaste lady immediately went to Vaikuṇṭha in the vehicle of (Lord) Viṣṇu made with foremost gems and accompanied by the courtiers of (Lord) Viṣṇu.

23. The boy went away from the house of the brahmin along with the brahmins. The most compassionate brahmins imparted him knowledge about the principles of life.

24. The brahmin boys left the child and returned to their place. The most wise child stood on the charming banks of the Ganges.

25. After bathing there he repeated the formula of Viṣṇu that was imparted by the brahmin and that is capable of dispelling hunger, thirst, disease and grief and is very difficult to get in the *vedas.*

26. The boy practised ascetic exercises at the bottom of the holy fig tree in the great forest and remained there for a long time.

Śaunaka said :

27. What excellent formula relating to (Lord) Hari was obtained by the wise boy ? You are fit to describe me.

Sauti said :

28. The formula consisting of twenty-two syllables and very difficult to find in the *vedas* was imparted graciously by (Lord) Kṛṣṇa to (Lord)Brahmā at Goloka in the past.

29. (Lord) Brahmā imparted that with devotion to Kumāra (Sanatkumāra), the intelligent one. O Brahmin ! That formula was imparted by Kumāra to the child.

30. *Om śrīm* obeisance to the venerable Lord of the dance circle- This formula is a wish-yielding tree.

31. The use of the hymn on the Supreme Being and the amulet described (by me) earlier for meditation has been explained in the Sāmaveda.

32. For meditation the form of a circle of splendour resembling the radiance of a crore suns is desired for ascetic practices by the ascetics, hosts of accomplished ones and gods.

33. The *vaiṣṇavas* meditate an extremely attractive, indescribable, charming form that is at the centre of this (lustre).

34-43. One has to meditate the paramount Lord, the Supreme Being having a dark complexion like the fresh cloud, the eyes like the autumnal lotus, the face resembling the autumnal full moon, the lips (red) like the ripe *bimba* (fruit), charming rows of teeth humiliating the rows of pearls, a gentle smile with the flute being supported by the hand holding it, the beauty of a crore god of love. He is an abode of divine sport, who is charming, who is furnished with the radiance of a lakh moons, who is an embodied being endowed with well-furnished (goddess) Śrī, who has the three folds (bends at the head, waist and leg), who has two hands, who wears the yellow dress, who is adorned with the gem-studded bracelet, armlet and anklet, whose region of cheeks shine with a pair of gem-studded pendants, whose head is adorned by peacock feather, who is adorned with a gem-studded garland, who is graceful with the garland of *mālatī* (flower) extending to the knee, who had besmeared with sandal paste all over the body, who favours the devotees who had the region of chest made shining by the excellent *kaustubha*[3] gem, who is always beheld with their bashful eyes by permanently youthful cowherdess surrounding him always and adorned with ornaments, who rests on the chest of Rādhā, who is worshipped, saluted and extolled by (Lords) Brahmā, Viṣṇu, Śiva and others, who is a young boy, who is the consort of Rādhā, who has a tranquil form, who is above the highest, who is unstained, who is of the form of a witness who is without any quality and who is above nature.

44. O Sage ! I have described you the (process of) meditation, hymn and the amulet. The use of the formula is true and the formula is a wish-yielding tree.

45. O Śaunaka! Now you listen to the story of the boy. The boy practised meditation for thousand divine years without food and emaciated belly.

46. Endowed with energy and being nourished by the efficacy of the accomplished formula, the boy beheld the divine world and a child in his meditation.

47-50. He was seated on a gem-studded throne and adorned with gem-studded ornaments. He was tender in age. He was dark. He wore the dress of a cowherd. He had a smiling face. He was surrounded by cowherds and cowherdesses. He was wearing a yellow dress. He had two arms. He had the flute in his hand. He had besmeared his body with sandal paste. He was being extolled by (Lords) Brahmā, Viṣṇu, Śiva and others.

He was above the supreme. After beholding the tranquil one for a long time, the tranquil son of the cowherdess discontinued (the meditation) when he was not able to perceive him and felt grief-stricken. That child wept at the bottom of the fig tree when he did not behold the boy.

51. Then there was a voice from the sky(containing) true, awakening, beneficial and measured syllables addressed to the weeping boy :

52. The form which you had beheld once will not be preceived by you again now. It cannot be visualised by people attached to worldly objects and bad ascetics.

53. After you shed your present mortal coil and gain a divine body, you will again perceive Govinda (grazer of cows), the destroyer of birth and death and (Lord) Hari.

54. After having heard these words, the boy ceased (crying) and rejoiced. In due course he discarded his body at a sacred place remembering (Lord) Kṛṣṇa in his heart.

55. The drums sounded in the heaven. There was a shower of flowers. The great sage Nārada was released from the curse.

56. Discarding the body, that soul got merged in the frame of (Lord) Brahmā. He became eternal from the olden time, when the distinction of time had disappeared.

57. O Śaunaka ! The manifestation and disappearance of eternal beings are at their will. There is no birth, death, decrepitude and disease for the devotees.

CHAPTER TWENTY-TWO

The Etymology of the Names of the Sons of Brahmā

Sauti said :

1. After the lapse of some interludes of *kalpas*, in the process of creation by (Lord) Brahmā, he (Nārada) had his birth from the throat (of Brahmā) along with the sages Marīci and others.

2. He was named as Nārada as he had his origin from the throat of (Lord) Brahmā. That excellent sage was hence known as Nārada.

3. The son, a foremost sage, who had his origin from the cetas (mind) of (Lord) Brahmā was named by Brahmā as *pracetas.*

4. The son that suddenly came into being from the right side of Brahmā, was proficient in all acts and hence was glorified as Dakṣa.

5. The word kardama is clearly found in the *vedas* in (the sense of) shadow. The boy had his origin from the shadow (of Brahmā) and hence glorified as kardama.

6. (The word) marīci is clearly found in the *vedas* as a variety of *tejas* (radiance). As he was born at once as extremely radiant, he was hence glorified as Marīci.

7. As the boy had performed a host of rites in his previous birth, he was called by the name Kratu even now as the son of Brahmā.

8. The principal organ of (Lord) Brahmā is his mouth from which a boy was born. (The word) *iraḥ* is an expression denoting 'radiant'. Hence he was designated as Aṅgirāḥ.

9. O Śaunaka ! (The word) *bhṛgu* has the meaning extremely radiant. As he was born at once as extremely radiant, he was hence known as Bhṛgu.

10. A boy born ruddy with much radiance was glowing with perpetual celibacy and hence designated as Aruṇi.

11. As the souls of the ascetics were under his influence by means of asceticism, the great ascetic boy was known as Haṁsī.

12. As soon as the boy was born, the disciple was under his control and hence that one very dear to (Lord) Brahmā was known as Vaśiṣṭha.

13-14. The boy whose effort was always in penance, was known as Yati, as he had restrain in all acts. (The word) *pula* is used in the *vedas* in (the sense of) penances and *ahaḥ* in (the sense of) explicit. The boy was known as Pulaha as the hosts of penances were explicit. In whom there was *pulaḥ*— a collection of penances of previous births and hence the boy who is of the form of multitude of penances was Pulastya.

15. (The syllable) *tri* (denotes the three qualities of *prakṛti* and (the syllable) a, (Lord) Viṣṇu. The boy having equal attention towards them is known as Atri.

16. As there are five matted hair on the head in the form of the flame of the fire born from the radiance due to penance, (the boy) was known as Pañcaśikha.

17. As he performed penance in an island country in another birth, the child was known by the name *Apāntaratamā*.

18. One who accomplishes himself the penance, and would enable others to reach and is capable of carrying on the penance is hence said to be Voḍhu.

19. O Sage! The boy who is always radiant on account of penance and lustre and whose mind likes to do penance, is hence known as Ruci.

20. Those who came into being at the time of the wrath of the creator (Brahmā) are known to be eleven. They are (known as) *rudras* on account of weeping and hence they were angry.

Śaunaka said :

21. I have a misapprehension that a boy among the *rudras* is Maheśa. You know the essence of the *purāṇas*. You are fit to remove my doubt.

Sauti said :

22-23. (Lord) Viṣṇu with the quality of *sattva* is the protector. (Lord) Brahma with the quality of *rajas* is the creator. Those the *rudras* with the quality of *tamas* are unavoidable and dreadful. Kālāgnirudra is the destroyer. One among them, a part manifestation of Śaṅkara is of the form of *śuddhasattva* (pure goodness). He is auspicious and a conferrer of auspiciousness for the pious.

24. The others are the digits of (Lord) Kṛṣṇa. Those parts of Viṣṇu and Śaṅkara are equal and are the forms of *sattva* (goodness) of the whole one.

25. O Brahmin ! I have described you (this) at the time of the origin of *rudra*. How have you forgotten ? All have been deluded by illusion. There is mental delusion even for the sages.

26. Sanaka, Sananda, Sanātana the third and the venerable Sanatkumāra the fourth are the sons of (Lord) Brahmā.

27. (Lord) Brahmā asked the first (born) sons to create and they did not concede. (Lord) Brahmā hence became angry. O Sage ! The *rudras* came into being from the wrath.

28. The two Sanaka and Sananda are expressions of happiness. The two boys were always cheerful and full of devotion.

29. Sanātana is Lord Kṛṣṇa himself, eternal and full. Truly the devotee of the lord is equal to him. Hence the boy was known as Sanātana.

30. The word '*sanat*' is an expression (meaning) 'eternal' and '*kumāra*' an expression (meaning) 'child'. Hence this one was designated as Sanatkumāra by (Lord) Brahmā.

31. O Sage ! I have described you the etymologies (of the names) of the sons of (Lord) Brahmā. Now you listen to the story of Nārada in order.

CHAPTER TWENTY-THREE

The Dialogue between Brahmā and Nārada

Sauti said :

1. O Śaunaka ! (Lord) Brahmā after having assigned all the boys the functions of creation, directed Nārada to do the creation.

2. (Lord) Brahmā told Nārada well-versed in the *vedas* and *vedāṅgas* (accessory texts to the *vedas*) words beneficial, true, constituting the essence of the *vedas* and leading to happiness.

Brahmā said:

3. O Child Nārada ! Foremost in the scion ! Dear to my life! One that causes the destruction of the darkness of ignorance with the flames of the lamp of knowledge. Come here.

4. Among all those to be respected, the father is the supreme preceptor. The two-one imparting knowledge and the other the mystic formulae are both equal and above the father.

5. O Son ! I am your father— the giver of knowledge and protector. By my command and to please me you take a bride.

6. He is said to be a disciple as well as a son who carries out the command of his preceptor. It is not for the welfare of an ignorant person who does not execute the words of the preceptor.

7. He is said to be learned, wise, prosperous and meritorious who acts as per the words of his preceptor. Such a person becomes prosperous at every step.

8. A householder is meritorious and prime among all the stages of life. An abode endowed with wife, children and grand children is the fruit of one's penance.

9. Just as the cows (go to the trough) for drinking water, all the manes come to the householder in the lunar fortnight[1] and the gods on the lunar days.

10. The householders perform the (rites) *nitya* (daily), *naimittika* (obligatory performed on specific occasions) and kāmya (for gaining desired fruits) always. This merit (confers) happiness in this world and enjoyment of heaven in the other world.

11. A householder who practises his duties would be liberated while living, famous, meritorious, glorious, wealthy and happy.

12. Whoever is famous and glorious is always (considered to be) living even though dead. One who is bereft of fame and glory is dead even though living.

13. After hearing the words of (Lord) Brahmā, Nārada, the foremost sage, spoke with modesty and fright and parched throat, lips and palate.

Nārada said:

14. Once on account of wordy quarrel between the father and son, there was injury leading to much ill-fame on account of fate.

15. I have been born as a *gandharva* and *śūdra* and had the respective functions. You were also not worshipped in this mundane world on account of my curse.

16. O Brahmā ! I have become free from the curse and you will also become free (from the curse). Quarrel is always considered as leading to a blemish and not to a quality.

17. One who induces me to have firm devotion to the lotus feet of lord Kṛṣṇa is my father, preceptor, kinsman, son or lord.

18. He truly is a father, a mine of compassion, who dissuades the children from the evil path followed by them on account of ignorance.

19. Which father would dissuade the son from devotion to the feet of (Lord) Kṛṣṇa and make him indulge in other matter?

20. Taking a bride is only for grief and not for happiness. It is an obstruction to the acts of penance, heaven, devotion, and emancipation.

21. O Brahmā ! Foolish householders have three kinds of wives—1) a chaste wife 2) enjoyable (prostitute) and 3) unchaste woman. All of them are intent on their selfish ends.

22. The chaste woman always serves her husband for the fear of the next world, for the sake of fame in this world and gratification of her desire.

23-24. The enjoyable always seeks pleasure and has only gratification of her desire. She serves her husband always for the sake of enjoyment. She will be enjoyable, dear and submissive as long as she is getting dress, ornaments, pleasure and excellent food from the husband.

25-27. The unchaste woman will ruin the family like the fire-brand. She is hypocritic serving the husband and serves not out of devotion. Being afflicted by passion she always desires the union with a male. She desires for fresh paramours more than the food. O Dear ! She desires to kill her husband for the sake of the paramour. A stupid person who trusts her, his life is worthless.

28. I have described to you the three kinds of wives—excellent, mediocre and lowest. (Even) the learned seekers of knowledge do not understand their minds.

29-30. The heart (of women) is like the edge of a razor and the face has the beauty of the autumnal moon. The speech is sweet like the nectar for accomplishing their desire. When (they are angry) they are equal to venom. Trusting them leads to universal destruction. Their intention is difficult to be known. Their action is totally concealed.

31. Immodesty is always their towering strength. Blemish and conceit reign supreme. Their trickery is unsurpassable.

32-33. O Preceptor of the Universe ! Their passion is eight times, food twice, harshness four times, and anger and perseverance six times than that of men. O Pitāmaha (Brahmā)! What consideration in this (matter) where there are a host of defects ?

34. What sport and what happiness for men in the abode of ordure, urine and impurity ? One's lustre gets lost in sexual union and decay of fame in conversation during the day.

35. There is destruction of wealth in excessive affection and the destruction of the body in excessive attachment. One's valour is lost in the company and destruction of one's prestige in quarrel. In placing faith (in them) there is destruction of all things. O Brahmā ! What happiness (there is) in (the company of) women ?

36. A man is able to make a woman submissive as long as he is wealthy, lustrous, prosperous and competence.

37. A wife looks at a sick, poor and old (husband) as an enemy and would feed him a little being afraid of the worldly practice.

38. O Brahmā ! Thus I have described the nature (of women). O Omniscient one! You know everything because you amuse in yourself.

39. O Lord ! Bless me and confer knowledge on me now. I seek devotion towards (Lord) Kṛṣṇa from you, the supreme wish-yielding tree.

40. After having spoken thus, Nārada held the lotus feet of the father and entreated his permission for undertaking auspicious penance.

41. After placing the palms together, the body bent on account of devotion and after doing circumambulation and prostration to (Lord) Brahmā, (Nārada) was about to go.

42-43. O Sage ! The creator of the world wailed aloud like an ordinary human being on beholding his son going away. He held him by the hand, embraced him and kissed him again and again. After having held him close to the chest for a long while, (Brahmā) placed him on his knees.

44. Lord Brahmā, who amuses in his own self and who is the preceptor of the preceptors of foremost ascetics, was not able to bear that separation similar to separation unbearable for men.

45. O Śaunaka ! Being afraid of separation from the son and deluded by the veil of (Lord) Viṣṇu, (Brahmā) addressed his son and began to speak overwhelmed by grief.

CHAPTER TWENTY-FOUR

The Dialogue of Brahmā and Nārada about Mundane Existence

Brahmā said :

1. O Child ! You go away for (doing) penance. What have I to do with worldly affairs ? I will go to Goloka for comprehending Lord Kṛṣṇa.

2-5. The sons Sanaka, Sananda, Sanātana, the third and the dispassionate Sanatkumāra, the fourth, Yati, Haṁsī, Āruṇi, Voḍhu and Pañcaśikha are all ascetics. What have I to do with worldly affairs ? Among all the sons Marīci, Aṅgiras, Bhṛgu, Ruci, Atri, Kardama, Pracetas, Kratu, Manu and Vasiṣṭha are always obedient to me. Others are imprudent and disobedient. What have I to do with worldly affairs ?

6. O Child ! You know from me. I will tell you the auspicious words mentioned in the Vedas and tradition yielding four-fold purposes of human existence.

7. All learned men desire for virtue, wealth, pleasure and emancipation laid down by the *vedas* and glorified by the sages in the assemblies.

8. What is laid down in the *vedas* is virtue. The contrary is unrighteous. At first a brahmin puts on the sacred thread and enjoys happiness.

9. Then he learns the *vedas* and pays the fees to the preceptor. Then he should marry a modest girl from a noble family.

10. One who is bent on serving her husband is said to be chaste and born in a good family. An immodest girl will never be born in a good family. How could crystal have its origin in a mine of rubies ?

11. O Nārada ! One who is born in a bad family on account of the defects of her parents is immodest, wicked and independent in all her actions.

12. O Child ! All wives are not wicked. They are a part of (goddess) Lakṣmī. Unchaste women born in the bad families are part of a celestial nymph.

13. A pious (lady) would serve and extol her husband devoid of qualities. An unchaste one would not serve her husband having good qualities and would censure him.

14. A pious person should make good effort to marry a girl from a good family. He has to retire to do penance at old age after having produced children through her.

15. It is better to live in fire, or in the mouth of a serpent or in a thorny place. Dwelling with a bad woman causes more grief than these.

16. You have learnt the Vedas from me. O Son ! You pay me the fee for the preceptor in the form of marrying a girl.

17. O Child ! Sinless one ! You marry Mālatī, born in a good family and your wife in former (birth) and do this auspicious thing on a good day.

18. That pious lady has taken her birth for your sake in the house of Sṛñjaya, born in the line of Manu, and is doing penance in Bhārata.

19. You take this excellent garland (Mālatī) set with gem representing a part manifestation of (godess) Lakṣmī (as your wife). The penance of people in Bhārata would not go without the fruit.

20. One should first become a householder, then a forest-dweller and then an ascetic for the sake of (gaining) release. This order (of life) has been known from the scriptures.

21. The worship of (Lord) Hari is the penance prescribed for the Vaiṣṇavas (devotees of Viṣṇu) in the scriptures.

22. You are a Vaiṣṇava. You be a householder and do worship of the feet of (Lord) Kṛṣṇa. O Son ! For a person having (Lord) Hari inside and outside (his mind) what is the need for doing penance.

23. O Sinless one ! For a person not having (Lord) Hari inside and outside (the mind), what use of doing any penance. (Lord) Hari is to be propitiated by penance. There is no other (way).

24. Wherever service has been done to (Lord) Kṛṣṇa, that is supreme penance. O Child ! On my words you become a householder and worship (Lord) Hari.

25. O Foremost sage ! You become a householder, for a householder is always happy. Enjoying the pleasant company of women is considered to be equal to enjoying pleasures in the heaven.

26. Those who aspire for redemption desire to behold and touch them. Touching the women gives much pleasure than touching any other thing.

27. O Sage ! Beholding and touching the child gives much more pleasure than that. The wife is dearer than all other things and hence she is declared as the beloved.

28. The wife is a means for begetting children and hence the son is dearer than hundred wives. There is no one greater than the son. No one is dearer than the son.

29. People may desire to have victory over others, but defeat only from the son. Wealth is not dearer than one's self and this son is dearer than that.

30. Hence one has to entrust with the son and the wealth that is his outstanding self. O Śaunaka ! After having spoken thus Brahmā stopped. Then Nārada, the foremost among the wise, spoke to his father.

Nārada said :

31. The father who urges his son in the unrighteous path after having known everything in scriptural knowledge, how could he be a compassionate one ?

32-33. All this mundane existence is perishable like the bubble of water. O Brahmā ! Just as a line on water is false, the three worlds (are false). (It is folly to) discard service to (Lord) Hari and have fickleness of mind in worldly matter. It is difficult to be born as a man. It should never go fruitless.

34. In this ocean of mundane existence which woman is dear to whom ? Who is a son or who is a kinsman ? Union is with waves of action and disunion is their removal.

35. Whoever makes one do good act is his friend, father and preceptor. One who induces another to have a bad thought would be an enemy. How could he be a father ?

36. O Father ! Thus I have described you the laws based on the scriptures. Even then your command has to be honoured.

37. O Venerable one ! I will first go to the hermitage of Nārāyaṇa. After listening the story of Nārāyaṇa I will take a wife.

38. After having stated thus the sage stopped talking in front of the father. That moment itself there was a shower of flowers on him.

39. After having stood for a while in front of his father, Nārada, the foremost sage, spoke again words of the scriptures yielding auspiciousness.

Nārada said:

40. Impart me the formula of (Lord)Kṛṣṇa that my mind had desired and the knowledge relating to that and the description of his qualities.

41. After that I will take a wife for your satisfaction. When one's mind is completely satisfied, he does work cheerfully.

42. After hearing the words of Nārada, the delighted lotus-born (Brahmā) again spoke to his son, the foremost among the learned.

Brahmā said :

43. A wise person should not receive the mystic formula from the husband or the father. Mystic formula (received)from men in different *āśrama* (states of life) does never yield happiness.

44. Men gain a formula, preceptor, husband, wife, knowledge, happiness, fear and grief not by their will but by destiny.

45. Maheśvara (Śiva) is your preceptor in the previous birth and our old (preceptor). O Child ! Go to (Lord) Śiva, the tranquil conferrer of good who is the preceptor of the wise.

46. Hence after receiving the formula and wisdom from the ancient one and listening to the story of Nārāyaṇa you come quickly to my abode.

47. O Śaunaka ! After having spoken thus, the supporter of the world stopped (talking). The sage after bowing to his father with devotion repaired to Śivaloka (the world of Lord Śiva).

CHAPTER TWENTY-FIVE

Nārada's Visit to Kailāsa

Sauti said:

1. In a trice the foremost brahmin went with delight to the beautiful and big abode of (Lord) Śiva extending a lakh yojanas

above Dhruva (the pole-star) built with enormous precious gems.

2. It was without any support and held by (Lord) Śiva by means of his ascetic strength. It was quite strange and abound with various temples. It was beheld by the holy aspirants and was abound with foremost ascetics and auspicious.

3. O Sage ! It was devoid of the rays of the sun and moon and was surrounded only by the fire in the form of walls with innumerable increasing glowing flames.

4. The excellent city was extending to a lakh yojanas and was always endowed with three crores of excellent gems. It was shining with varied charming pictures inlaid with superb diamonds.

5. O Brahmin ! It was endowed with mirrors made of rubies and pearls not even could be dreamt and decorated by Viśvakarmā (the divine architect). O Śaunaka ! It was always attended to by the devotees of (Lord) Śiva.

6. It was endowed with hundred crore lākhs of accomplished persons, three crore lakhs of his courtiers and three lakhs of dreadful Bhairavas (a class of attendants on Śiva) and surrounded by four lakhs hundreds of sacred places.

7. It was always surrounded by celestial trees and flowering excellent *mandāra* trees. It was shining with beautiful *kāmadhenus* (celestial cows) similar to the sky (made beautiful) by hundreds of cranes.

8. The sage was surprised to behold all these at Mānasa. (He thought) what is impossible for the preceptor of the celestial ascetics ? That world was different from the three worlds and it dispelled fear, death, disease, affliction and decrepitude.

9. He beheld (Lord) Śiva at a distance at the centre of the assembly. He was tranquil, conferrer of auspiciousness and charming. He had the three lotus eyes. He had the five moon-like faces. He was holding the Ganges (on the head). He had the spotless crescent on the head.

10. That master had the matted hair resembling the heated gold. He was nude (had the quarters as the dress). He was

white, endless and without decay. He was muttering with delight the name Kṛṣṇa with the garland made of the seeds of the lotus in the Ganges.

11. He had a beautiful blue throat. He was adorned by the foremost serpent. The most excellent one was worshipped by the foremost ascetics, accomplished persons and sages. He was the master of the accomplished souls. He was the cause of giving perfection. He was the conquerer of death. He was the destroyer of *kāla* (Time) and *yama*.

12. He was charming with a pleasant and smiling face. He was the conferrer of auspiciousness and favours on all the (people of) the universe seeking him. He was always quickly appeased. He was devoid of the disease of mundane existence. He was dear to the devotees. He was the sole kinsman of the devotees.

13. The sage went near the trident-bearer (Śiva) and bowed to him with his head with horripilation on his body. Playing on the three-stringed lute he sang again and extolled (Lord) Kṛṣṇa with his sweet voice.

14. Beholding that smiling son of Brahmā who is a foremost sage and an outstanding among the knowers of the *vedas*, Lord (Śiva) looked up from his seat with delight along with the foremost ascetics, accomplished souls and great sages.

15. He hurriedly offered the sage an embrace, best wishes, seat etc. O Śaunaka ! He enquired the sage the purpose of his auspicious visit and the progress of his penance.

16-17. (Lord) Śiva sat on an excellent, beautiful gem-studded throne along with the foremost courtiers. O Brahmin ! The son of Brahmā did not sit down. He bowed to the lord with palms held together and extolled him with devotion. Nārada extolled (Śiva) with the pleasing hymn, conferring good and composed by the *gandharva* king, saluted again and sat on the left side of (Lord) Śiva at his command.

18. He then conveyed his mental desire to (Lord) Śiva, the person that fulfills one's desire, there itself. The mine of compassion after having heard the words of the sage quickly promised and said yes.

CHAPTER TWENTY-SIX

The Dialogue between Śiva and Nārada about Daily Practices

Sauti said :

1. The divine sage requested (Lord) Śiva for the hymn on (Lord) Viṣṇu, the amulet, formula, the supreme mode of worship, (mode of) meditation and wisdom.

2. Lord Śiva imparted him the hymn, amulet, formula, (process of) meditation, mode of worship and the wisdom preceding it.

3. The foremost sage after having gained everything and his ambition being fulfilled spoke with devotion after saluting the preceptor who is fond of the devotees.

Nārada said :

4. Foremost among the knowers of *veda*! You describe me the daily practices of the Brahmins leading eternal protection of one's own duties.

Śrī Maheśvara said :

5-7. One should get up at the *brāhma muhūrta*[1] and contemplate his preceptor as having the explaining posture of hand with a cheerful and smiling face, fond of the disciples, gracious looking, tranquil, constantly pleased and as the form of brahman itself in the spotless, undecaying subtle thousand-petalled lotus in the *brahmarandhra* (aperture in the crown of the head) after discarding the night dress.

8. After having contemplated thus and worshipping the preceptor in the spotless white lotus in the heart, one should contemplate the favourite deity in the extensive heart lotus.

9. One should contemplate that god in the (prescribed) method of contemplation. After taking his permission one has to do the appropriate work.

10. After contemplating, saluting and worshipping the preceptor in the prescribed way, one should then get his command, contemplate and worship the favourite deity.

11. The preceptor makes manifest the deity, formula, mode of worship and the muttering (of a formula etc.). The deity does not make the preceptor manifest. Hence the preceptor is greater than the deity.

12-13. The preceptor is (the lords) Brahmā, Viṣṇu and Maheśvara, *prakṛti* (*Primordial Nature*), Īśa and others, moon, fire, sun, wind, Varuṇa (god of ocean and upholder of righteousness), mother, father and friend. The preceptor is the Supreme Brahman. No one is superior to the preceptor to be adored.

14. If the favourite deity is angry the preceptor is capable of protecting him. But if the preceptor is angry all the gods are not capable of protecting him.

15. If the preceptor is pleased, one would always have success at every step. But if the preceptor is displeased, everything gets destroyed always.

16. The ignorant person who by mistake worships the god (first) without worshipping the preceptor, there is no doubt that the sinner gets the sin of killing hundreds of brahmins.

17. Lord Viṣṇu himself has declared thus in the Sāmaveda. Hence the preceptor is more adorable and superior to the favourite deity.

18. O Sage ! The aspirant after having contemplated and extolled his favourite preceptor, should reach a clean place and happily answer the calls of nature.

19-24. Water, (ground) near water having holes, the vicinity of animals, near a temple, the roots of a tree, the pathway, a ploughed land, a field of crops, cow-pen, the river-bed, a flower garden, muddy place, inside a village, near the house of men, a post, a bridge, a bush of reeds, the cremation ground, the presence of fire, a playing ground, a great forest, beneath the bed-stead, a place having the shades of trees, an air hole with a living being inside, a place abound with *dūrvā* (grass), a place abound with *kuśa* (grass), an ant-hill, a place for growing trees and a place got ready for (performing) rites are to be avoided and one should answer the call of nature in a pit dug up devoid of sun's heat.

25. The calls of nature should be done facing the east during the day, facing the west during the night and facing the south during the twilight period.

26. While passing stool one should keep silent and restrain the breath so that the smell may not enter (the nostril). After nature call a wise man should cover it with mud and then purify himself.

27. One should purify first with earth and then with water. Now you listen to me about the quantity of mud and water to be used (for purification).

28. (After passing urine) one has to apply mud once to the penis and four times to the left hand or two times to each hand. This is said to be purification after urination.

29. If the urination is after copulation it is two fold. Or if purification after urination is done after copulation, it is fourfold.

30-31. Application of earth is done once to the penis, thrice to the anus and ten times to the left hand and seven times to both the hands. The feet becomes pure after (application) six times. This is the (mode of) purification after passing stools for the brahmin householders. For widows two-fold purification has been laid.

32. For ascetics, *vaiṣṇavas*, a realised ascetic and unmarried persons four times that of the householders has been laid down.

33. A twice-born until he is not initiated, a *śūdra* and a girl have to purify till the bad smell is erased.

34. The purification for the *kṣatriyas* and *vaiśyas* are the same as that of the Brahmin householders. For *vaiṣṇavites* and anchorites it is two-fold (that of the above).

35. A person desirous of purity should not increase or decrease (the prescribed quantum) of purification. If there is any violation of the laid down rules, one has to do expiation.

36. Now you attentively hear from me about the purification and the rules (governing it). A *brahmin* becomes purified by mud purification and impure if violated.

37-39. One should avoid mud that is from the ant-hills, dug up by rats, in the midst of water, the remnant of previous use, from a dwelling place, from a place of calamity, having a living being inside, dug up by the plough, from the root of the *kuśa* grass, from the root of the *dūrvā* grass, obtained from the root of the holy fig tree, is got from the bed-stead, from the cross-roads, from the cowpens and that is from the grazing grounds.

40. One should avoid mud from a field of crops and the gardens. A brahmin becomes pure by (these) purifications irrespective of whether he has bathed or not bathed.

41. One devoid of purification is always impure and is unfit (to do) all religious rites. After doing the purification as laid down, the learned brahmin has to rinse his mouth.

42-43. After purifying his mouth by gargling sixteen times, one should brush his teeth with the twig used as toothbrush. One should again gargle sixteen times for purity of his mouth. O Nārada ! Listen to me about the rules governing the twigs used as tooth-brush.

44-48. It has been laid down by (Lord) Hari in the Sāmaveda dealing with the daily practices. One should avoid the twigs of *apāmārga*, *sindhuvāra*, *āmra*(mango), *karavīraka*, *khadira*, *śirīṣa*, *jāti*, *punnāga*, *śālaka*, *aśoka*, *arjuna*, *kṣīrivṛkṣa*, *kadambaka*, *jambūka*, *bakula*, *tokma*, *palāśa*, *praśastaka*, *badarī* (jujube), *pāribhadra*, *mandāra*, *śālmali* (silk cotton), thorny trees and creepers, *pippala*, *priyāla*, *tintiḍīka* (tamarind), *tālaka* (palm), *kharjūra* (date), *nārikela* (coconut) and *tāla* (palmyra). One who is devoid of purity of teeth is devoid of all purities.

49. One who is devoid of purification is always impure and is not eligible for all religious rites.

A brahmin would become pure after doing purification and after wearing washed clothes.

50. After washing the feet and sipping (water thrice) one should perform the morning twilight (worship). A brahmin born in a good family would thus do the twilight (worship) in the three twilight (periods).

51. One who performs the three twilight (worships) is deemed to have bathed in all the sacred waters. One who is

devoid of the three twilight (worships) is not eligible for all religious rites.

52. One who performs a rite during the day will not reap its fruits if he does not perform the morning and evening (twilight worship).

53-54a. He is to be expelled like a *śūdra* from all the rites of a brahmin. A brahmin who discards the morning, midday and evening twilight (worships) would incur everyday (the sin) of killing a brahmin or committing suicide.

54b-55a. A brahmin who is devoid of (practising) the *ekādaśī* (fasting on the eleventh day of a fortnight) goes to (the hell) *kālasūtra* for a *kalpa* (period) just like the Vṛṣalīpaki (a low caste man).

55b-57a. After having performed the morning twilight (worship) in this way one should salute his favourite preceptor, tutelary deity, Sun, Brahmā, Īśa, Viṣṇu, *māyā* (illusion), Padmā (Lakṣmī) and Sarasvatī and then one should touch the preceptor, clarified butter, mirror, honey and gold. The most pious aspirant should do bathing etc. at the appropriate time.

57b-58. When one bathes in the *puṣkariṇī* (tank) or a well, the pious and wise person should first lift five balls (of mud). One should bathe in the male or female river[2], cavern or sacred water.

59-65. O Sage ! One desiring the satisfaction of Lord Kṛṣṇa has to do the resolve after bathing and then bathe again. The resolve destroys the sins committed by the great *vaiṣṇavas* and householders. After doing the resolve, the brahmin should besmear the mud on the body with the following formula from the *vedas* for the sake of purifying the body: O mud! You are traversed by the horse, chariot and by (Lord) Viṣṇu. You bear the wealth. You take away my sin and the evil deeds I have done. You have been lifted up by Lord Kṛṣṇa as a boar with hundred hands. Climb upon my body and release me from all my sins. O Most Fortunate One ! You confer on me merits. You permit me to bathe. After having stated thus and standing in the water upto the navel and preceded by the formula, one has to make an auspicious circle extending to four cubits. O Ascetic ! One has to invoke the sacred waters therein by touch. I will tell you (now the names of) the sacred waters.

66-71. O Ganges ! Yamunā, Godāvarī, Sarasvatī, Narmadā, Sindhu, Kāverī ! You be present in the water. Nalinī, Nandinī, Sītā, Mālinī, flowing into the ocean ! The Ganges rising from the feet of (Lord) Viṣṇu and flowing in three courses ! Padmāvatī, Bhogavatī, Svarṇarekhā, Kauśikī, Dakṣā, Pṛthvī, Subhagā, Viśvakāyā, Śivāmṛtā, Vidyādharī, Suprasannā, Lokaprasādhini, Kṣemā, Vaiṣṇavī, Śāntā, Śāntidā, Gomatī, Satī, Sāvitrī, Tulasī, Durgā, Mahālakṣmī, Sarasvatī, Rādhā dearer than the life of Kṛṣṇa, Lopāmudrā, Diti, Rati, Ahalyā, Aditi, Saṁjñā, Svadhā, Svāhā, Arundhatī, Śatarūpā, Devahūti and others should be remembered.

72. After bathing repeatedly and becoming much pure, the wiseman has to wear the mark at the root of his arms on the throat and chest.

73. Bathing, charity, penance, oblation, rites relating to gods and manes all these would be fruitless without a mark on the forehead.

74. A brahmin should wear the mark and do the twilight (worship) and water oblation. After having saluted the gods with devotion one should go home with delight.

75. After washing the feet and wearing washed clothes, a wise man should enter the temple. (Lord) Hari has stated thus.

76. Whoever enters a temple without washing the feet after bathing, his bathing and other five actions such as muttering, oblation and the like are lost (become fruitless).

77. If householder enters the house after wearing a wet dress, goddess of fortune curses him cruelly and leaves the house angrily.

78. The brahmin who washes his leg from the ankle to the knee, he becomes a *cāṇḍāla* till he beholds the Ganges.

79. O Brahman! An aspirant should be seated on a seat, becoming pure and sipping (water), should offer worship with devotion and restraint as laid down in the *vedas.*

80. The worship of (Lord) Viṣṇu in the *śālagrāma*[3] in the gem, in the formula, in the image, in water, on the ground, on the back of a cow, in the preceptor and in a brahmin is commendable.

81. O Nārada ! Among all the things worship in the śālagrāma is commendable. It is said to be presided over by all the gods.

82. A person who sprinkles with *śālagrāma* water (water used for anointing the *śālagrāma*) is deemed to have bathed in all the sacred waters and initiated in all the sacrifices.

83. Whoever drinks with devotion the śālagrāma water daily, he becomes liberated while alive and finally reaches the abode of (Lord) Kṛṣṇa.

84. O Nārada ! Wherever there is the disc mark on the *śālagrāma* stone all the sacred waters and the lord certainly remain there with the disc.

85. An embodied person dying there consciously or unconsciously on account of fate would reach the place of Lord Hari mounted on (a chariot) made of gem.

86. Which pious person would worship (Lord) Hari (Viṣṇu) elsewhere except at śālagrāma? By the performance of the worship of (Lord) Hari there, one would get the full benefits.

87. I have described you the substratum for the worship. You listen to me about the mode of worship. I will describe you the (mode of) esteemed worship of (Lord) Hari according to the scriptures.

88. Some *vaiṣṇava* makes a present to (Lord) Hari sixteen beautiful and pure nice ties daily with devotion (as explained below).

89. Some (offer) twelve articles and some others five. It depends on one's resources and devotion is the basic factor in worship.

90-91. Seat, dress, water for washing the feet, water offered for sipping (for reception), water offered for sipping, flower, sandal paste, incense, lamp, offering of excellent eatables, fragrant articles, garland, excellent and graceful bedstead, water, food and betel along with the substratum shall be offered.

92. Except fragrant articles, food, bed and betel the materials are twelve. Water for washing the feet, water for sipping for reception, water for sipping, offering of eatables and flowers are the five (items).

93. The foremost aspirant should offer all these items together with the basic (formula). The basic (formula) imparted by the preceptor is commended in all the rites.

94. After performing the purification of the elements at first, (one has to do) the *prāṇāyama* (regulated breathing) then. (One has to do) then the assignment of the major and minor limbs and the assignment of the sacred formula.

95. After completing the assignment of the letters, one has to dedicate the *arghyapātra* (vessel for holding water offered for reception). After drawing a triangular figure one should worship the tortoise therein.

96. A brahmin should fill the conch with water and place it there. After having worshipped the water, one should carry and bring the sacred waters.

97. One should again sprinkle that water on the materials for worship. After taking flower (in the hand) then, one should be seated in the meditative posture after becoming pure.

98. One should then meditate (Lord) Kṛṣṇa with the mode of meditation imparted by the preceptor without distraction of mind. After meditation, the aspirant should offer the water for washing the feet etc., with the basic (formula).

99. Then one has to worship the gods presiding over the minor and major limbs and (Lord) Hari. After muttering the basic formula according to one's ability, one should request the formula of the god to leave.

100. After having made different presents and extollation one has to read the amulet. Then after making good for omission, one has to prostrate with the head (touching) the ground.

101. A wise man should perform the sacrificial rite after worshipping the god. O Sage ! One should then make the offering in the śratuta (relating to scriptures) and smārta (relating to codes of law) fires.

102. One has to perform the daily srāddha (rite for the ancestors) according to one's capacity with charity corresponding to one's wealth and then the virtuous doer should bring it to a close. This is the order as heard from the scriptures.

103. Thus I have told you everything as prescribed in the *vedas.* Do you wish to hear more about the daily practices of the brahmins ?

CHAPTER TWENTY-SEVEN

The Instruction about Daily Practices

Nārada said :

1-2. O Lord ! Kindly tell me everything about what is to be eaten and what is not to be eaten, what is to be done and what is not to be done and what is to be enjoyed and what is not to be enjoyed by the brahmin householders, ascetics, *vaiṣṇavas,* widows and unmarried persons (first state of life).

Maheśvara said :

3-4. Some brahmins are ascetics, some are sages abstaining from taking food, some others consume the wind, some others eat fruits, some others take food at the proper time being householders in the company of their wives. O Brahmin ! Their tastes and desires are varied.

5. The food fit for oblation is always commended for brahmin householders. The remnants (of food dedicated to lord) Nārāyaṇa (Viṣṇu) is desirable. Whatever has not been offered (to God) should not be eaten.

6. The food and water not offered to (Lord) Viṣṇu are ordure and urine respectively. Food (eaten) on the day dedicated to (Lord) Viṣṇu (the eleventh day of a fortnight) is always ordure and urine.

7. A brahmin who wilfully eats the food on the day dedicated to (Lord) Viṣṇu, there is no doubt that he enjoys the sin committed in the three worlds.

8. O Nārada ! Food should not be eaten (repeated thrice for emphasis) by brahmin householders when the day dedicated to (Lord) Viṣṇu (*ekādaśī*) comes.

9-10. A householder, a śaiva (devotee of Śiva), *śākta* (devotee of goddess) and a brahmin devoid of knowledge go to *kālasūtra* (a hell) after eating on the day dedicated to (Lord) Viṣṇu. He remains there being bitten by insects measuring (the size) of rice and eating the ordure and urine till (the periods of) fourteen Indras.

11. Whoever eats on the *janmāṣṭamī* (the eighth day of a fortnight on which Lord Kṛṣṇa was born), the *rāmanavamī* (the ninth day of a fortnight on which Lord Rāma was born) relating to (Lord) Viṣṇu and Śivarātri (the night on the fourteenth day dedicated to Lord Śiva), he also incurs sins twice as much.

12. If a person is not capable of abstaining from food he may eat fruits and roots and drink water otherwise he would become a suicide when he sheds his mortal coil (by fasting).

13. By eating once the food offered as oblation for (Lord) Viṣṇu, one would not earn the sin of omission and he would get the fruits of fasting.

14. A brahmin householder fasting on the *ekādaśī* (eleventh day dedicated to Lord Viṣṇu) in Bhārata would remain in Vaikuṇṭha for a period of the age of Brahmā.

15. O Nārada ! This has been told for the Śaiva and Śākta householders and especially for the *vaiṣṇavas*, ascetics and *brahmacārins* (those in the first stage of life).

16. He is said to be a *vaiṣṇava* who partakes daily the offering made to (Lord) Viṣṇu. (Such a person reaps) the benefit of hundreds of fasting. He gets redeemed in his life-time.

17. The sacred waters and all the gods desire to touch him. Holding conversation and beholding such a person destroys all the sins.

18. (Partaking) cooked rice or parched grain twice (in a day) is deemed to be alright in some regions. But it is not highly commendable for brahmins either for eating or for offering to god.

19. O Brahman ! It is not certainly forbidden like the betel not to be eaten by ascetics, widows and *brahmacārins* (those in the first stage of life).

20. O Foremost Brahmin ! Betels for widows, ascetics, *brahmacārins* and *tapasvins* (doers of penance) is certainly like the beef.

21. O Nārada ! You now listen to me about what is not to be eaten by all brahmins as described in the Sāmaveda by Lord (Viṣṇu) on the daily practices.

22-23. Drinking milk from a copper vessel, the consumption of ghee which is a remnant of that eaten by others, (drinking) milk together with salt, eating of fresh beef, drinking of coconut water from a bell-metal, honey kept in a copper vessel[1] and sugarcane juice kept in copper vessel are no doubt equal to wine.

24. A brahmin drinking water after lifting up water with the left hand is known to be drinking wine. He is excluded from all religious duties.

25. The remnant of food eaten should never be offered to Lord Hari. O Sage ! The remnant of water drunk is like beef.

26-27. *Vāningaṇa* fruit in (the month of) Kārttika (November-December) is known to be beef. Mūlaka in (the month of) Māgha (January-February), *lambi* in śayana (*ekādaśī*), white coloured palmyra, *masūra* and fish are to be avoided by all the brahmins in all the regions.

28. A brahmin who eats fish wilfully has to fast for three days. He becomes pure after doing expiation.

29. Eating pumpkin on the new moon days destroys wealth. One will not remember (Lord) Hari after eating *bṛhat* on the 2nd day (of a fortnight).

30. Eating *paṭola* is forbidden as it causes the growth of the enemy. Eating *mūlaka* on the third and fourth days (of a lunar fortnight) causes destruction of wealth.

31. Eating of bilva on the fifth day causes a blemish. Eating of nimba on the sixth day would make one born as a bird.

32. Eating of palmyra by men causes the growth of disease. Moreover eating palmyra on the seventh day would destroy the body.

33. The eating of coconut on the eighth day destroys the intellect. (Eating of) *tumbī* (bottlegourd) on the ninth day and *kalambīkā* on the tenth day (is considered to be equal to eating) beef.

34. One should not eat *śimbi* (kidney bean) on the eleventh day, *pūtikā* (pot herb) on the twelfth day and brinjal on the thirteenth day as it would cause loss of children.

35-36a. O sage ! Eating of blackgram on the fourteenth day is a great sin. So also is the eating of meat on the new moon or full moon day for the householders. Meat sprinkled with water may be eaten by householders on other days.

36b-37. O Nārada ! While bathing in the morning or at the time of annual rite for the dead ancestors, or at *pārvaṇa* (offering oblations to the manes on the eighth or fourteenth day) or on the day of an austerity or on the new moon or full moon day or at the time of the transit of the sun from one constellation to another, or on the fourteenth or eighth lunar days (the use of) mustard oil or boiled oil is commended.

38. Sexual intercourse, use of sesamum oil, (eating) meat, *raktaśāka* (a kind of vegetable) and eating in bell-metal are prohibited on a Sunday or at the time of annual ceremony for the dead ancestor, or on the day of an austerity.

39. (On the eleventh day) sleeping (during the day) and (eating) the consecrated meat of a tortoise are prohibited. So also having copulation with one's wife during the day is prohibited for all the castes.

40. Partaking curd in the night, sleeping during the twilight periods or during the day and having copulation with the women in menses are all the cause for (going to) hell.

41-43. One should not eat food from a woman in her menses, a childless widow and a prostitute. The food from a śūdra, the food from a sacrificer, the food from the *śrāddha* (rite for the dead ancestor) (performed) by a *śūdra* are also forbidden. O Brahmin sage ! The food from a *vṛṣalīpati* (low caste man) (is also forbidden). O Brahmin ! The food from an usurer and an astrologer are forbidden. The food from an *agradānidvija* (a brahmin who accepts presents in honour of the dead) or a physician (is prohibited). The oil used for taking hand-sketch should not be eaten.

44. Eating meat in (the asterisms) *mūla, mṛga* and *bhādrapada* is equal to beef. Shaving is prohibited on the new moon day and (the asterism) *kṛttikā* for brahmins.

45. If one makes offering to the gods or manes after copulation or shaving, the water offering would become blood and the giver would go to hell.

46. What could be done and what could not be done, what could be eaten and what could not be eaten I have told you everything. What more do you desire to hear ?

CHAPTER TWENTY-EIGHT

He Form of Brahman, Vaikuṇṭha, etc.

Nārada said:

1. O Jagannātha (Lord of the universe)! O Preceptor of the world ! I have heard everything by your favour. You kindly describe the form of Brahman that determines Brahman.

2. O Lord ! Master ! Whcthcr Brahman is corporeal or incorporeal ? Is it a quality or not a quality ?

3. Is it perceptible or imperceptible ? Is it united in the embodied beings or not ? What are its essential features ? What has been determined in the *śāstra* or *veda* ?

4. Is primordial nature different from Brahman or of the form of Brahman? What are the essential characteristics of the primordial nature as known from the scriptures ?

5. O Omniscient one ! Is it pre-eminent in creation and which of the two is pre-eminent—all these you examine mentally and describe me firmly.

6. After hearing the words of Nārada, the venerable five-faced one smiled and began to expound the nature of the Supreme Brahman.

Mahādeva said :

7. O Dear Nārada ! What esoteric and excellent knowledge you had asked is very difficult to get from the *vedas* and *purāṇas.*

8. I, Brahmā, Viṣṇu, Śeṣa, Dharma, Mahạt, Virāṭ— all these, O Sage, have been determined by us in the *vedas.*

9. O Foremost among the knowers of the Vedas ! That which is endowed with a quality, which is visible and apparent to the senses, we have ascertained it in the *vedas.*

10. You listen to me. I will describe you a little of what (Lord) Viṣṇu explained in Vaikuṇṭha when he was requested by Dharma and Brahmā.

11-12. It is the essence of all the principles. It is the eye for those made blind by ignorance. It is the lamp that dispels the delusion caused by erroneous cognition of the duality (of nature). It is of the form of Supreme Brahman. It is eternal. It remains in all the bodies. It is of the form of a witness of all actions as being present in all the bodies.

13. (Lord) Viṣṇu himself is the five vital airs, Brahmā, the lord of the beings (is) the mind. I am the form of all knowledge. The primordial nature is the energy that governs.

14. We are all subject to the Supreme Being. When he remains we remain, when he goes we also go after him just like the attendants (following) a monarch.

15-16. The individual soul is his reflection and the enjoyer of all actions. It is like the image of the Sun and Moon in pots filled with water. Just like the image getting merged in the Sun and Moon when the pots are broken, the individual soul also merges in the (Supreme) Brahman when there is dissolution.

17. O Dear one ! When the universe is destroyed, the Supreme Brahman alone remains. We all, the universe, the movables and immovables get merged in it.

18. It is a circular luminous form. It has the lustre resembling innumerable mid-day Suns of the summer.

19. It is extensive like the sky, all pervasive and undecaying. It is easily perceptible by the ascetics like the disc of the moon.

20. The ascetics refer to it as the eternal Supreme Brahman. They contemplate that truth, the wholesome auspiciousness day and night.

21-22a. He is desireless, without form, Supreme soul and the lord. He is an embodiment of free-will. He is independent. He is the cause of all causes. He is of the form of Supreme Bliss. He is the cause of Supreme Bliss. He is supreme, prime, first being, without quality and above the primordial nature.

22b-25. O Sage ! The primordial nature of the form of the source of all gets merged in it only just as the power to burn rest in the fire, lustre in the Sun, whiteness in the milk, coldness in water, sound in the sky and smell in the earth. Moreover, the Brahman is devoid of quality and the primordial nature is also devoid of quality. For the purpose of creation that Brahman itself is known to be the *puruṣa* (the first being) as a part manifestation. He himself is endowed with qualities. He is known to be the unmodified knowledge.

26-28. The *prakṛti* possessing three qualities is remembered to be a shadow of the Supreme. Just as the potter is able to make the pot with the earth, that Brahman is capable of creation with the (help of) *prakṛti*. Just as the goldsmith is able to do the pendant with gold, the Brahman also is also (able) to create with her (*prakṛti*).

29. The things created by the potter are not permanent. But the mud is permanent. The article made by the goldsmith are not permanent. But the gold is permanent.

30. That Supreme Brahman as well as the primordial nature are permanent. Some people say that both of them have an equal superiority.

31. The potter and goldsmith are capable of bringing together mud and gold respectively. But the mud and gold are not capable of securing them.

32. O Nārada ! Hence the Brahman is greater than that primordial nature. Some people say that their eternity is certain.

33. Some people say that the Brahman itself is the primordial nature as well as the pumān(first being). Some others hold that the primordial nature is different from the Brahman.

34. That Brahman is the Supreme abode and is the cause of all the causes. O Brahman ! That is the characteristic of the Brahman. This has been known from some scriptures.

35. Brahman is the soul of all (the beings). It is unstained and is of the form of a witness. It is omnipresent and is the first being. This characteristic has been known from the scriptures.

36. The nature that is the energy of that Brahman, is of the form of all and is the source of all things and from which that Brahman possesses energy. This is the characteristic of nature.

37. The ascetics always contemplate that Brahman of the form of lustre. But the *vaiṣṇavas* who are my devotees and who have subtle intellect do not think so.

38. They ask how that wonderful light could be adored without some Being (that holds it). How can there be an effect without a cause on the earth ?

39. Hence the *vaiṣṇavas* always contemplate there a beautiful form of a being, an embodiment of free-will and of the same form as one's soul.

40. There is an eternally concealed place by name Goloka of the shape of lustrous circle having the radiance of a crore suns.

41. It is quadrangular extending to a lakh crore *yojanas* and charming. It is built with precious gems. It is abound with cowherdesses.

42. It is lovely, circular in form like the sphere of moon. It is set with different kinds of gems. By His will it is without any support.

43. It is fifty crore *yojanas* above Vaikuṇṭha. It is full of cows, cowherds and cowherdesses. It is endowed with the wish-yielding tree.

44. O Sage ! It is filled with divine cows and abound with the dancing circle. It is covered by the *vṛndāvana* forest. It is surrounded by (the river) *virajā*.

45-46. It has the Śataśṛṅga (mountain) glowing with the radiance of gold. It has the desired prosperity. It has lakh crore of beautiful hermitages. It has hundred mansions. It has a beautiful hermitage. It is endowed with walls and moats. It has the *pārijāta* forest.

47. It is extremely radiant with the excellent *kaustubha* gem. It has extremely gracious steps set with exquisite diamonds.

48. It has doors set with foremost gems and endowed with mirrors. The hermitage therein has been beautified with many kinds of varied pictures.

49-50a. It has sixteen doors illumined by gem-studded lamps. That excellent lord stays in the beautiful gem-studded throne made of greatly valuable gems and various kinds of beautiful pictures.

50b-61. He is dark like the fresh cloud. He is a child of tender age. His eyes emit the lustre of the midday sun of the autumn. His face has the auspicious radiance of the autumnal full moon. His beauty excels the beauty of crores of gods of love. He puts to shame the lustre of crore moons. He is well-nourished. His body is united with that of the goddess of wealth. He is smiling. He holds the flute. He is glorified and auspicious. He shines with a pair of excellent yellow garment. His whole body is besmeared with sandal paste. He shines with the *kaustubha.* He is adorned with the garland of *mālatī* and wild flowers extending to the knee. His body has three bends. He is adorned with the gems and rubies. He has the peacock feather on his head. He shines with a crown studded with exquisite gems. He is made beautiful by the gem (studded) bracelets, armlets and anklets. His region of the cheeks are made beautiful by a pair of gem-studded pendants. He has a charming teeth resembling a row of pearls. His lower lip is like the ripe *bimba* (fruit). The elevated nose is graceful. He is looked at respectfully by the permanently young and smiling cowherdesses surrounding him all around. They are adorned with ornaments made of quality gems. He is cheerfully worshipped by the foremost gods, excelient ascetics, sages, kings, (Lords)Brahmā, Viṣṇu, Śiva, Ananta, Dharma and others. He is fond of the devotees. He is the lord of the devotees. He is the conferrer of boons on the devotees. He is the master of *rāsa* (dance). He is a connoisseur. He is enshrined in the chest of Rādhā. O Sage! the *vaiṣṇavas* contemplate such a form and the formless one.

62-64a. Our Supreme Lord, the master undecaying Supreme Brahman, the venerable one, the eternal one, embodiment of free will, one devoid of quality, one devoid of desire, one above the nature, one that is the support of all (the beings), one that is the source of all (the beings), omniscient, one that is all (things), the lord of all beings, one to be adorned by all, one that confers all perfections is to be contemplated always (by all the beings).

64b-66a. He himself (remains) as the venerable first person at the Goloka, with two arms, wearing the dress of a cowherd and surrounded by the cowherd courtiers, the whole being, endowed with prosperity (as) Lord Kṛṣṇa, the consort of Rādhikā. He is remembered as the inner soul of all the beings, perceptible everywhere and omnipresent.

66b-67. (The syllable) kṛṣ denotes 'all' and the syllable na expresses 'the soul'. As he is the Supreme Brahman, the soul of all beings, he is glorified as 'Kṛṣṇa'. (The syllable) kṛṣ denotes 'all' and the syllable na expresses 'the first'. The first being among all, pervading (everywhere) is hence glorified as 'Kṛṣṇa'.

68-69. He himself as a part manifestation (remains) at Vaikuṇṭha as having four arms. That lord of Kamalā (Lakṣmī) is surrounded by his courtiers possessing four arms. He is by his digit (manifestation) the protector and the lord of the world, (lord) Viṣṇu. He is the consort of the daughter of the ocean at Śvetadvīpa with four arms.

70. I have thus described you everything, about the form of the Supreme Brahman who is to be contemplated, served, worshipped and desired.

71. O Śaunaka ! After having spoken thus (Lord) Śiva stopped. Nārada extolled him with the hymn (uttered) by the *gandharva* king.

72. Becoming pleased with the eulogy of the sage the venerable first being (lord) Acyuta (Śiva), the conqueror of death, blessed him with the desired knowledge.

73. The foremost sage with a delighted face and look saluted him with reverence and then at his command departed for the hermitage of (lord) Nārāyaṇa, the house of merits.

CHAPTER TWENTY-NINE

The Query of Nārada about the Supreme Being Lord Kṛṣṇa

Sauti said:

1-4. The divine sage Nārada then beheld the wonderful hermitage of sage Nārāyaṇa endowed with the *jujube* forests, abound with different kinds of trees and fruits, resounding with the melody of male cuckoos, surrounded by elephants, lions and hosts of tigers, devoid of violence and fear on account of the glory of the foremost sage, the inaccessible forest more attractive than the heaven, abound with three crores of hermitages of the accomplished souls and ascetics and endowed with forests of sandal wood and *pārijāta* (trees).

5-6. The sage beheld that foremost sage in the middle of the court. He was attractive. He was seated on the gem-studded throne. He was the preceptor of the ascetics. He was muttering (the name) Kṛṣṇa, the Supreme Brahman, the soul and the lord. O Śaunaka ! The son of Brahmā saluted him after beholding him.

7. (Nārāyaṇa) rose up quickly, and blessed him after embracing. He then enquired about the welfare with affection. He then offered him the worship due to a guest.

8-15. He then made Nārada seated on an attractive gem-studded throne. After the fatigue of the journey was duly removed by being seated on the beautiful throne, (Nārada) spoke to that venerable eternal and foremost sage: O Lord ! After mastering at my father's place all the *vedas* which are difficult to understand, and after gaining knowledge from the foremost ascetic and the formula from (Lord) Śiva, my mind does not get pleased. My fickleness has not been removed. Being urged by the mind I have beheld your lotus feet. Now I would like to get some special knowledge (from you), whereby I could have the narration of the quality of (Lord) Kṛṣṇa that dispels birth, death and decrepitude. O Lord ! When do (Lords) Brahmā, Viṣṇu, Śiva and others, Indra and the gods, sages, Manus and the wise contemplate? From whom the creation proceeds ? In whom does it merge? Who is (Lord) Viṣṇu, the lord of all the beings, the cause of all creation? What is the form of that lord ? O Lord of the world! What is his task ? You deserve to describe me everything after deliberation.

16. After hearing the words of Nārada, the venerable sage smiled and began to narrate the meritorious legends that sanctifies the world.

CHAPTER THIRTY

The Eulogy Glorifying Lord Kṛṣṇa

Lord Nārāyaṇa said :

1. (Lords) Lambodara (Big bellied son of Śiva), Hari, Umāpati (Śiva, consort of Umā), Īśa, Śeṣa, Brahmā and others, the hosts of gods, Manus, the foremost sages, Vāṇī (Sarasvatī) Śiva (consort of Śiva), Tripathagā(Ganges flowing in three courses), Kamalā (Lakṣmī) and others should contemplate the lotus feet of the venerable lord.

2. One who desires to cross the deep and dreadful ocean of mundane existence, his limbs being surrounded by the serpents

in the form of the forest fire, and one who desires to become his servant should contemplate the lotus feet of the venerable one.

3. One has to contemplate the lotus feet of that venerable lord, glorious of lifting up the Govardhana (hill), that lifted up the distressed wet earth with the fore-part of his teeth and held the worlds in the pores of his skin.

4. One whose body has been pierced by fear and grief such as the birth, death etc., should contemplate the lotus feet of the venerable lord, Lord Hari, the creator, the originator of the *vedāṅgas* and *vedas* through the medium of the glory sung by the texts such as the *vedāṅgas* and *vedas.*

5. One should contemplate the lotus feet of the venerable lord, the honey bee hovering around the lotus face of the cowherdesses, the lord of *rāsa* (dance), the expert in the appreciation of art, Lord Viṣṇu who wanders in the Vṛndāvana in the dress of a cowherd.

6. The creator of the world (Brahmā) falls at the winking of his eye. O Darling ! Who is capable of describing his deeds? O Sage Nārada ! You also contemplate those lotus feet of (Lord) Hari with great regard.

7. You, we and the Manus and great sages are all a part of his part manifestations. Those who desire to cross the mundane existence are a part. The *mahat* and *virāṭ* are his parts.

8. The thousand headed one bears the universe in the region of the head as if it is equal to the mustard. The Śeṣa (supports) the tortoise just like a mosquito (holding) an elephant. The tortoise is a part of the digit of (Lord) Kṛṣṇa.

9. The blemishless fame of Lord of Goloka is not well-manifest in the scriptures and *purāṇas.* The *purāṇas* such as the Padma Purāṇa are not capable of describing. Worship that all-pervasive god glorified in the Padma (Purāṇa).

10. In all the universes there are always gods such as Brahmā, Viṣṇu and Rudra from that all-pervasive god. But their innumerable numbers, the scriptures and gods do not know him. You worship that Lord.

11. He creates Brahmā. Brahmā after making eternal the nature, the originator of the world, Brahmā and all others from the nature, worship the nature that yields devotion.

12. *Prakṛti* (Nature) is of the form of Brahman. She is not different from it. The Eternal being makes the creation through her. All the prosperities in the world are (created) by a part. All are deluded by her.

13. (Goddess) Nārāyaṇī is supreme, eternal energy of the Being, the Supreme Soul. The Lord of the soul possesses energy by means of her and is incapable of creation without her.

14. O Darling ! You go and marry. Now you have been sent to carry out the command of your father. You be worshipped everywhere as one honouring the command of the father. You be victorious always.

15. Whoever honours his wife with dress, ornaments, sandal paste etc., nature gets pleased with him just like (Lord) Kṛṣṇa when worshipped by a brahmin.

16. She is indeed of the form of the wife in every world by her illusion. If the wife is insulted, she would get humbled.

17. Whoever honours a divine woman having a husband and children, Nature, the conferer of all auspiciousness, gets worshipped by that.

18. The *mūlaprakṛti* (prime nature) is only one She is of the form of the whole Brahman. In creation that eternal illusion of Viṣṇu is of five kinds.

19. The goddess presiding over the life force of (Lord) Kṛṣṇa, the Supreme soul, is glorified as Rādhā, the most dear among all his consorts.

20. Lakṣmī, the consort of Nārāyaṇa, is of the form of all the wealth. Sarasvatī is the presiding deity over desires. She is to be worshipped.

21. Sāvitrī, the mother of the scriptures, is worshipped in the form of the consort of Brahmā. Durgā is the consort of Śaṅkara (Śiva). Gaṇeśvan (the lord of the attendants of Śiva) is her son.

NOTES

Chapter One

28.1. Normally oval in shape and obtained from the source of the Gaṇḍakī river in Nepal; worshipped as representing Lord Viṣṇu. Śalagrāma is the correct form.

49.2. See 28.1 above.

60.3 Puṣkara, near Ajmer in Rajasthan is the only sacred place having a temple for Brahmā.

61.4. This line '*nārāyaṇarṣirbhagvan pradadau naradaya ca*' omitted in the printed text has been added.

Chapter Two

6.1. A distance of eight or nine miles.

Chapter Three

9.1. The reading *śrīvidhi* has been amended as *śrīnidhi* cf. Viṣṇusahasranāmastotra. Verse 78

* This hymn is not found in one of the books.

59.2. A day of Brahmā consisting of 1000 yugas.

59.3. kṛta, tretā, dvāpara and kali respectively 1,728,000; 1,296,000, 864,000 and 432,000 years of men.

Chapter Four

11.1. The five shafts are mentioned differently as the flowers—*aravinda, aśoka, cūta, navamallikā* and *nīlotpala*.

27.2. They were Madhu and Kaiṭabha.

Chapter Five

25.1. Water offered to guests while receiving them.

Chapter Six

26.1. See Ch.3 verse 59.

Chapter Seven

4.1. The rivers flowing from west to east are female and those from east to west are male.

Chapter Nine

94.1. The reading '*candra*' to be amended as '*ardha*' to yield the correct sense.

Chapter Ten

17.1. A mixed tribe from a *kṣatriya* father and a *śūdra* mother.

90.1. The text here has omitted the *kāṁsyakāra* (bell-metal maker) cf. 10.20.

Chapter Eleven

7.1. The other reading *kalijāt* means that is on account of the *kali* (*yuga*).

19.2. *Ekādaśī* is a sacred day for Lord Viṣṇu. Fasting and devotion to Him on that day confers special merits.

32.3. A great sacrifice performed by a monarch at the time of his coronation as a mark of his undisputed sovereignty.

Chapter Thirteen

13.1. These are located about the pubis, in the umbilical region, in the pit of the stomach, in the root of the nose, in the hollow between the frontal sinuses and in the level of the brows respectively. See MW. p. 380 (under Cakra).

88.2. A posture of the fingers conducive for the meditative practices.

Chapter Fourteen

60.1. Respectful offering consisting of curd, clarified butter, water and honey.

Chapter Sixteen

32.1. The exact meaning of these two words are not known. They seem to denote hump on the back and elephantiasis.

69.2. A condiment consisting of ground coriander, mustard pepper, ginger etc.

69.3. Name of a tree.

Chapter Twenty-One

17.1. Refers to the four mind-born sons of Brahmā-Sanaka, Sananda, Sanātana and Sanatkumāra.

18.2. Consisting of curd, clarified butter, water, honey and sandal paste.

40.3. is the curl of hair on the chest of Viṣṇu, always referred to as a gem.

Chapter Twenty-Three

9.1. *Purvakāle* in printed text seems to be wrong. It must be *parvakāle* for correct sense.

Chapter Twenty-Six

5.1. The last part of the night and the early part of the day.

58.2. Rivers flowing in the east are female and those flowing in the west are male.

80.3. Stone obtained from the Gaṇḍaki river bed in Nepal worshipped as an emblem of Lord Viṣṇu.

Chapter Twenty-Seven

23.1. Laghu in the text seems to be a mistake for Madhu.